BIRD BOXES
AND
FEEDERS

BIRD BOXES
AND FEEDERS

Featuring 11 step-by-step
woodworking projects

S T E P H E N M O S S *WITH*
A L A N & G I L L B R I D G E W A T E R

NH
NEW
HOLLAND

First published in 2001 by New Holland Publishers (UK) Ltd

London • Cape Town • Sydney • Auckland

24 Nutford Place, London W1H 6DQ, United Kingdom
80 McKenzie Street, Cape Town, 8001, South Africa
Level 1, Unit 4, 14 Aquatic Drive, Frenchs Forest, NSW 2086, Australia
Unit 1A, 218 Lake Road, Northcote, Auckland

ISBN 1 85974 175 4

Editorial Direction: Rosemary Wilkinson
Project Editor: Kate Latham
Production: Caroline Hansell

Designed and created for New Holland by AG&G Books
Design: Glyn Bridgewater
Illustrators: Alan and Gill Bridgewater
Project design: Alan Bridgewater
Photography: Ian Parsons
Editor: Fiona Corbridge
Woodwork: Alan and Gill Bridgewater, William Del Tufo

Reproduction by PICA Colour Separation, Singapore
Printed and bound by Times Offset (M) Sdn. Bhd.

The information in this book is true and complete to the best of our knowledge.
All recommendations are made without guarantee on the part of the authors and the
publishers. The authors and publishers disclaim any liability for damages or injury
resulting from the use of this information.

Dedication

Alan and Gill would like to dedicate this book to cousin Colin and his wife Wynn
— both keen bird-watchers and wildlife gardeners.

CONTENTS

Introduction *6*

INTRODUCTION

Sometimes when we're walking in the countryside, we stop and sit down to watch birds for a while – a Robin pecking at the crumbs from our sandwiches, a thrush picking blackberries, a

Scraps of food left over from your picnic sandwiches are a guaranteed way of attracting a wide variety of interesting and unusual birds.

Kestrel hovering overhead, or perhaps even Swallows swooping and diving to catch flies. It's incredibly exciting to see the sheer variety of birds, their beautiful colours, and their fascinating movements. And then when we are in the workshop carving a slab of green oak, or whittling a stick with a knife, we marvel at the pure pleasure of creating objects from wood.

So there you have it... bird-watching and woodwork – two of the most popular hobbies of all time. This book has been written to share with you the joy of working with wood, and the delight of enticing birds into your

A bird bath is not only an attractive garden feature in its own right – watching the birds bathing is a fascinating and instructive way of learning about bird behaviour.

garden. It is for woodworkers who are interested in birds, and bird-watchers who want to build bird boxes in order to attract birds into

the garden. It features satisfyingly creative
woodwork, which brings with it the added bonus

*Building bird boxes and feeders
is a great way to spend your free
time; watching the birds use them
is an added pleasure.*

of encouraging a greater variety of birds into your garden, giving
you birdsong to listen to in the morning, and the enjoyment of
feeding birds in the winter... so much fun!

Part 1

BIRDS IN YOUR GARDEN

Birds *are some of the most visible and easily observed of all living creatures – and where better to watch their habits than in your own garden? By providing food and nest sites for birds, you can enjoy their antics and behaviour, as well as providing a valuable service for the birds themselves. In winter, the food we supply can mean the difference between life and death for small birds. In spring and summer, bird boxes can help many species to raise their families. We can watch and learn all year round.*

ATTRACTING BIRDS TO YOUR GARDEN

A carefully considered, well-designed, wildlife-friendly garden is a series of "mini habitats", each of which provides a relatively safe place for birds to feed, shelter, roost or nest. Large, mature trees attract woodland birds, flowering plants produce seeds and are a beacon for insects, herbaceous borders provide food and ground cover, while wide areas of lawn are ideal for the more adventurous feeders.

The hawthorn provides berries from late summer until the following April, making it a very valuable food plant for thrushes and Blackbirds.

Not all gardens are large enough to include all these habitats. But even the smallest urban plot can provide enough food and shelter to create a little oasis for the birds. Wherever you live, and irrespective of the size of your garden, you can do all sorts of things to make it appeal to your local birdlife. You'll be amazed at the difference a few simple adjustments can make.

Let part of your garden "go wild"

A neatly manicured garden, where flowers are deadheaded the minute they are past their best, and shrubs are clipped back with enthusiasm, is the last thing birds want. So allow at least part of your garden to "go wild", providing a wealth of seeds and insects for the birds to feed on, and a wider choice of places to nest and roost. If you're really keen, why not plant a wild flower meadow, using native seed varieties obtainable from reputable garden centres.

Plant "food plants"

Birds love berry-bearing plants such as elder, hawthorn, honeysuckle, cotoneaster, pyracantha and yew – and they're attractive to look at as well.

Put out food

A reliable supply of food can be the difference between survival and death for many small birds.

Provide water

Water is just as important as food, so treat the birds to a bird bath for washing and drinking.

Make a garden pond

If you have the room, another way to provide water is by making a pond. Ponds also encourage all manner of wildlife, another useful food resource for birds.

Bird heaven – not only does this garden have a bird bath, but it is sited in a pond – it's the perfect place for birds to drink, bathe and feed.

A design for a bird-friendly garden

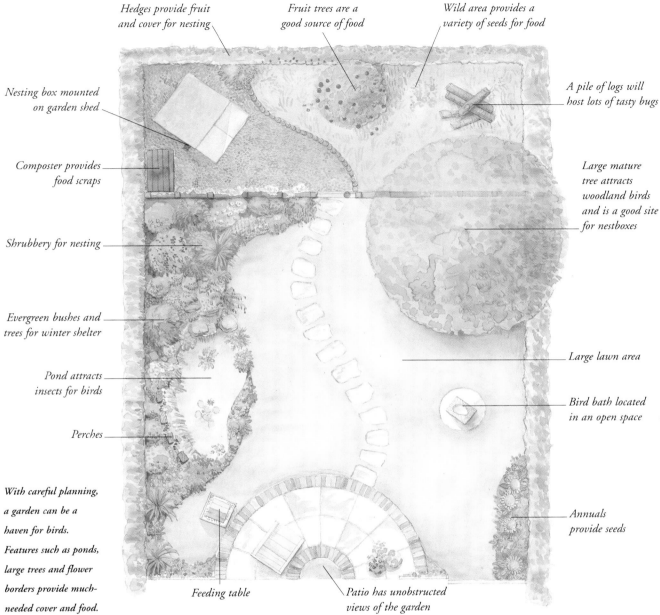

Hedges provide fruit and cover for nesting

Fruit trees are a good source of food

Wild area provides a variety of seeds for food

Nesting box mounted on garden shed

A pile of logs will host lots of tasty bugs

Composter provides food scraps

Large mature tree attracts woodland birds and is a good site for nestboxes

Shrubbery for nesting

Evergreen bushes and trees for winter shelter

Large lawn area

Pond attracts insects for birds

Bird bath located in an open space

Perches

With careful planning, a garden can be a haven for birds. Features such as ponds, large trees and flower borders provide much-needed cover and food.

Annuals provide seeds

Feeding table

Patio has unobstructed views of the garden

Plant shrubs and bushes for nesting
Some garden birds won't use nestboxes, but you can still help them by making sure your garden has a selection of dense shrubs where they can nest safely.

Keep out pests
Squirrels love bird food, so use squirrel-proof feeders. But the real villains are cats, which kill millions of birds. Turn to page 17 for ideas on minimizing this carnage.

Keep notes on what you see
Get a desk diary and note which birds you see, and when. Years later you can look back at your diary and draw pleasure from recalling long-forgotten sightings.

Enjoy the birds!
Gardening shouldn't be hard work all the time! Why not dig a little and then watch the birds… trim a little and then watch the birds… weed a little and then…

FEEDING GARDEN BIRDS

Providing a regular supply of different foods is one of the best ways of encouraging a variety of bird species to come into your garden. In Part 3 we look at a range of designs for bird feeders, from a simple peanut feeder to a really elaborate feeding station that will have the birds coming back for more. But before you get out the toolbox, read this section to discover which foods are suitable for stocking the feeder.

Feed regularly

There's nothing worse for the birds than discovering a garden full of food, then coming back a week later to find that the supply has run out. During the winter months especially, small birds need to feed almost every minute of the day during daylight hours, or they run the risk of starving to death. So once you start feeding them, don't stop.

Provide variety

Variety is the spice of life – for birds as well as humans. Different species have very different food requirements. Ideally you need to provide peanuts, seeds, grains, suet and other fat, fruit – such as windfall apples – and a variety of specialized foods, such as mealworms.

Keep it clean

Stale, leftover food can soon go mouldy, attracting pests and possibly causing disease, so make sure you clear away leftovers every couple of days, and give your bird table and feeders a good clean every few weeks.

Buy from a reputable source

Make sure the food you put out is suitable for wild birds by buying it from a reputable dealer (many do mail order) or from one of the bird protection groups. If the food is in any way less than perfect – stale, mouldy, sour, or tainted with chemicals – then reject it.

Bird feeders are an essential addition to the garden, especially during the winter, when they provide a valuable supplement to the birds' natural diet.

GOOD FOODS FOR GARDEN BIRDS

There is now a huge and somewhat bewildering variety of different foods available, from basic peanuts and seeds (which are suitable for a wide range of birds) to specialized foods for individual species. Some of the best foods are listed below. Apart from specially bought foods, kitchen scraps will go down well with your garden birds: anything from bread to bacon, cooked rice and grated cheese. Starlings are also partial to pet food! Fresh fruit is popular with Blackbirds, Starlings and thrushes. If you have doubts about the suitability of foods, then do not put them out.

Peanuts: *Make sure that you put them in a suitable feeder, so that small birds cannot choke on whole nuts. Use fresh raw (unroasted and unsalted) peanuts.*

Sunflower seeds: *Like peanuts, sunflower seeds are popular with a wide variety of birds. Some suppliers sell seed types to suit winter and summer feeding.*

Seeds and grains: *Seeds are the staple diet of many species, while grains tend to be the winter diet of woodland and farmland birds.*

Fat: *Specially designed food bars, containing insects, suet and other animal fats, are excellent energy-providers, especially in winter.*

Fruit: *Fresh fruit is popular with many birds. Apples, oranges, grapes, pears, plums and peaches are all a welcome addition to the diet.*

Leftovers: *Food scraps – bread, cooked rice, lentils, cheese and dog food – provide a good supplementary diet for a wide variety of bird species.*

NESTING AND NESTBOXES

A part from providing a regular supply of food and water, the next best thing you can do for your garden birds is to provide safe places to nest. Planting a good variety of trees, bushes and shrubs will provide natural nest sites, but you can help even further by putting up nestboxes. Nestboxes are simply an artificial way of creating a nest site for birds that normally nest in crevices or holes in trees.

Natural nest sites are in relatively short supply, and competition means that many birds fail to find a place to nest. By designing and building nestboxes – and mounting them on buildings or trees correctly (positioning is important) – we are offering a safe and convenient, much-needed alternative.

Nestboxes also look attractive, especially if you make them yourself and spend time and trouble at all stages. The boxes described in the following projects are carefully designed and easy on the eye – great fun to make and good for the birds.

Nestbox designs

Nestboxes come in all shapes and sizes (see Part 3). An open-fronted box is suitable for species such as the Robin or Pied Wagtail. A box with a small entrance hole will accommodate species such as Great and Blue Tits, House and Tree Sparrows. Other designs include a chimney box (made from a hollowed-out piece of wood) for Tawny Owls, and a wedge-shaped box for Treecreepers.

Once you've made your nestbox, it must be sited in the best place to attract birds. It will also need yearly maintenance to keep it in good condition.

FOUR TYPES OF NESTBOX

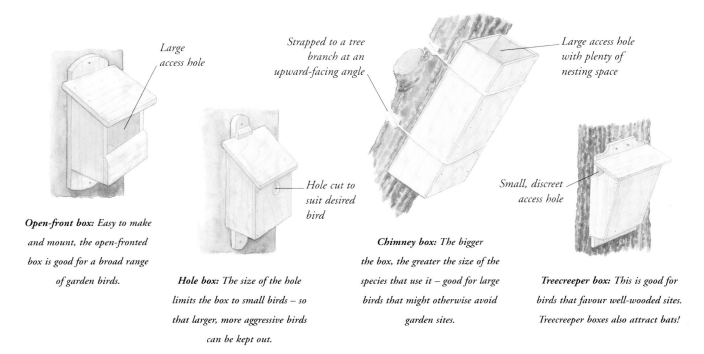

Large access hole

Strapped to a tree branch at an upward-facing angle

Large access hole with plenty of nesting space

Hole cut to suit desired bird

Small, discreet access hole

Open-front box: *Easy to make and mount, the open-fronted box is good for a broad range of garden birds.*

Hole box: *The size of the hole limits the box to small birds – so that larger, more aggressive birds can be kept out.*

Chimney box: *The bigger the box, the greater the size of the species that use it – good for large birds that might otherwise avoid garden sites.*

Treecreeper box: *This is good for birds that favour well-wooded sites. Treecreeper boxes also attract bats!*

Nestbox maintenance

Once the breeding season begins, it is best to leave the box well alone, as too frequent inspections can cause the parent birds to desert. However, once the eggs are being incubated you may make the occasional quick check – just to make sure that all is well.

After the chicks have fledged and left the nest, give the box a good clean, removing any old nesting material and scrubbing with soap and hot water.

With luck, a well-considered, beautifully made and carefully positioned box will provide an excellent home for birds year after year, and give you and your family hours of pleasure watching their breeding activities.

Nestboxes should be sited carefully: the box on the left is too low and in full glare of the sun, so would not be suitable for nesting birds.

Siting a nestbox

A nestbox should always be fixed to a firm base: either a wall, tree, fence or post. Height is not critical, but it should normally be at least 1.5 metres above the ground. Don't put the box too high, or you will be unable to reach it easily for maintenance.

Direction is important: baby birds can fry in hot sunshine, so it's best to site the box in the shade, preferably facing in any direction between north-east and south-east. Try to keep the box away from thick foliage or other places that would make it easy for predators to gain entry. Don't put boxes too close to each other, as birds will fight other birds entering their territory.

PESTS AND PREDATORS

*I*t can sometimes seem as if your garden is a battleground between squabbling birds, pesky squirrels and murderous cats. In many ways that's a fair picture: nature truly is "red in tooth and claw", even within the cosy confines of the garden, when food is at stake. If we provide a fast-food restaurant and hotel for the birds, we shouldn't be surprised if less welcome visitors abuse our hospitality.

PESTS

Let's start with garden pests such as aphids, slugs and caterpillars, the bane of many a gardener's life. Here you have two choices: either smother your plants with pesticides and slug killer, or try a less aggressive approach, encouraging natural predators such as ladybirds, frogs and toads into the garden. Remember that birds themselves help get rid of pests: Song Thrushes make short work of slugs, while many species of bird will take caterpillars, especially during the breeding season.

If you do decide to use sprays and chemicals, then at least try to use the more eco-friendly varieties, obtainable from reputable garden centres.

Squirrels can make short work of traditional bird feeders, ripping them apart to get to the contents. One solution is to use squirrel-proof feeders.

Many birds will eat the slugs and snails that can wipe out a vegetable crop.

A wildlife garden should always have room for beneficial insects. These seven-spot ladybirds are hibernating inside the seedhead of this plant.

Larger pests include rats and mice, which feast on spilled food from feeders and bird tables, making it essential that you clean up as often as possible. But perhaps the most annoying mammal of all is the one known affectionately as the "American tree rat" – the grey squirrel.

Squirrels are among the most agile, acrobatic and ingenious of all animals, and are particularly partial to peanuts. One way to foil their efforts is to construct a squirrel-proof feeder (see page 50), which lets the smaller birds in while keeping the squirrels at bay. Nestboxes should also be protected, as far as possible, from attack by marauding squirrels, which are always on the lookout for a tasty snack of eggs or chicks.

CATS

The world seems to be divided into two camps: people who love cats, and people who don't. Oddly, the first camp also includes many millions of people who love birds. These kind souls often encourage birds to come into their garden for food and shelter where they are in danger of becoming dinner for their own pet cat!

Cats are responsible for countless millions of bird deaths each year – so how do you protect the birds that you are attracting to your own garden? Well, if you don't like cats, you can buy a device which emits a high-pitched sound unbearable to a cat's ears which will keep them out of your garden area. But if you or your neighbour owns a cat, this may not be a practical option. Bells round a cat's neck are fairly ineffective, though perhaps a really large, loud one will give some warning.

Generally, you must remember to site your bird feeders and bird baths in a relatively open space, so that cats are not able to creep up easily on birds while they are feeding or bathing. Nestboxes should be fairly safe, but make sure that they are not sited too near the ground or close to convenient branches if fixed to a tree.

BIRD PREDATORS

A final word on bird predators such as Jays, Magpies and Sparrowhawks. Many people consider these to be the real villains of the bird world: they are ruthless predators that kill millions of songbirds. Although these species do kill smaller birds, we should remember that this is their purpose in life. Predators and prey have a balanced relationship, in which numbers of the latter generally regulate populations of the former.

There are many reasons why bird predators have increased in recent years, not least the welcome reduction in shooting and the banning of pesticides such as

DDT. In some ways, we are responsible for attracting these birds into our gardens: after all, by providing plenty of food we attract artificially high concentrations of small birds, which make easy pickings for predators. We must also remember that most songbirds will die before they reach a year old, and falling prey to a Sparrowhawk is at least a quick and natural way to die – unlike being tormented by a well-fed domestic cat. So you can experience the spectacle of one of the bird world's greatest hunters without guilt.

There are cat lovers and there are bird lovers.
I would reckon that this fat cat is a bird lover!

Part 2

MATERIALS, TOOLS AND TECHNIQUES

Building bird houses, boxes and feeders from wood is a rewarding and therapeutic activity... but only, it must be said, if you are using the appropriate tools, materials and techniques. It doesn't matter if you only have a small working area, as long as you have a workbench and a few carefully selected tools. Whether you're an expert or a novice, this section will show you the way.

MATERIALS

While all manner of materials could undoubtedly be used to build bird houses and feeders — such as plastics, metal or concrete — we prefer to use wood from sustainable sources in conjunction with acrylic paint and basic hardware. We feel that these materials are, to a great extent, "green" — non-toxic, non-polluting, biodegradable and easy to work with — altogether man- and bird-friendly.

SOME OF THE MATERIALS YOU WILL NEED

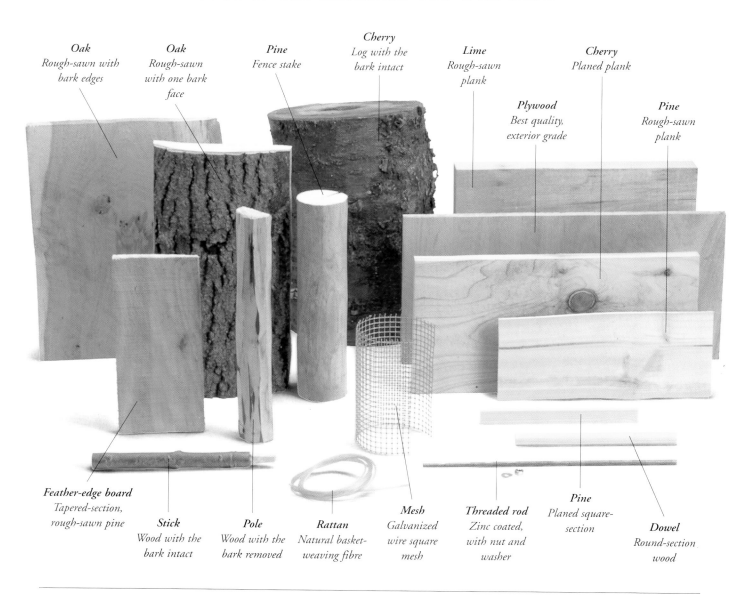

Oak
Rough-sawn with bark edges

Oak
Rough-sawn with one bark face

Pine
Fence stake

Cherry
Log with the bark intact

Lime
Rough-sawn plank

Cherry
Planed plank

Plywood
Best quality, exterior grade

Pine
Rough-sawn plank

Feather-edge board
Tapered-section, rough-sawn pine

Stick
Wood with the bark intact

Pole
Wood with the bark removed

Rattan
Natural basket-weaving fibre

Mesh
Galvanized wire square mesh

Threaded rod
Zinc coated, with nut and washer

Pine
Planed square-section

Dowel
Round-section wood

TIMBER

We always advocate using exterior-grade plywood and various easy-to-find, sustainable native woods – cherry, oak, ash, pine and lime – either as rough-sawn planks, or as in-bark (barky) slab wood. The best source for rough-sawn planks and barky wood is the sort of operation that sells fence posts, bean poles, garden timber and logs. The wood is usually sold "as is" – meaning you turn up, look the wood over, and choose the piece that suits. You will often find that the supplier directs you to a stack of heavy, wet wood piled high in a forest clearing, so wear stout footwear and old clothes, and take thick gloves to protect your hands. Remember that when buying barky wood, the wider the slab, the thicker the piece. Also, as barky wood is the first slice from the log, it will be wildly waney-edged (the uncut edge of the board will be curved). Study the working drawings, and be ready to modify the projects to suit the available wood.

HARDWARE

While all the projects demand exterior-grade screws and nails – so, in theory, you could use brass or aluminum – our preferred choice is steel, either plain or galvanized. The mix of rough-sawn wood, barky green slab wood, painted and rubbed plywood, dully gleaming galvanized nails, and wood streaked with rust, all makes for an aesthetically pleasing whole. As to whether or not you decide to use flat-headed nails, or nails with heads that can be driven below the surface, it really depends on your choice of wood. If you feel that the wood is likely to split, or the bark will slip off, then flat-headed nails are best. Screws can be either slot-headed or cross-headed, as long as the length and diameter fit the bill.

When using wire mesh, we always choose a good-quality galvanized square-grid mesh, on the grounds that it is easy to work and structurally strong in its own right. If the fixings fail, then the rigid gridded mesh usually stays put much better than woven mesh.

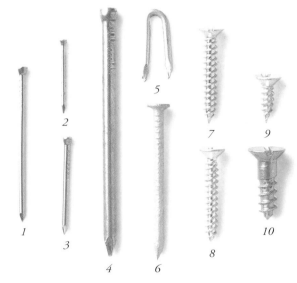

*A selection of the pins, nails, staples and screws needed for making the projects is shown above: **1.** Panel pin, bright steel, 40 mm; **2.** Panel pin, bright steel, 20 mm; **3.** Panel pin, bright steel, 25 mm; **4.** Round-headed nail, bright steel, 70 mm; **5.** Staple, galvanized, 18 mm; **6.** Flat-headed nail, galvanized, 40 mm; **7.** Slot-headed screw, zinc coated, 25 mm; **8.** Cross-headed screw, zinc coated, 25 mm; **9.** Slot-headed screw, zinc coated, 12 mm; **10.** Slot-headed screw, bright steel, 18 mm.*

PAINTS AND GLUES

The primary concern is that the paints and glues should be non-polluting, low-odour and non-toxic. We have opted for using water-based acrylic paints, varnishes and glues, which can be used without wearing a face-mask. The brushes are easy to wash, and most importantly of all, these materials are safe for the birds. Apart from using minute amounts of artist's oil paint, we avoid petrochemical paints.

TOOLS AND TECHNIQUES

*T*hese projects will supply you with lots of juicy woodworking tasks – sawing, nailing, sanding, painting, and so on – all of which are enjoyable. But the whole construction process is so much more of a pleasure when you use the correct tools for the job, and have a clear understanding of the basic techniques.

MEASURING AND MARKING

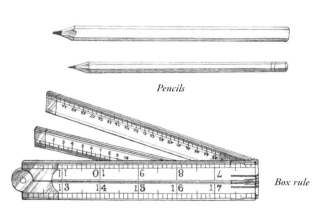

Pencils

Box rule

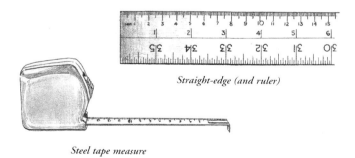

Straight-edge (and ruler)

Steel tape measure

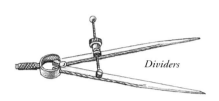

Dividers

Compass

Compass and dividers

Though a compass is primarily used for scribing out circles, while dividers are used for reading and transferring measurements, both tools are, to a great extent, interchangeable. We tend to use a compass for setting out circles on plywood and doing the more delicate working drawings. We prefer to use dividers for transferring measurements and drawing circles on rough-sawn wood – simply because they are more robust and can survive the wear and tear of woodworking.

Try square

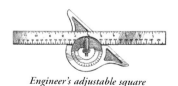

Engineer's adjustable square

Pencil, ruler, straight-edge and tape measure

For all woodwork that starts with measurements and drawn lines, you will need a selection of pencils, a ruler, a straight-edge, and a measuring tape. A good set-up would include hard and soft pencils for drawing directly on to the wood, a box rule for small, precise measurements, a metre-long steel rule that doubles up as a straight-edge, and a steel tape measure for measurements greater than a metre. Because products come from all over the world, it's a good idea to use rulers that combine both metric and imperial gradations.

Square

Woodwork is an ongoing procedure of testing that lines and edges are at right angles to each other. If you need to set out a corner, or check that one edge is true to another, then you must use a square. While a traditional steel and wood try square can be used for most tasks, an all-metal engineer's adjustable square can be used both for straightforward squaring, and for drawing out all the angles through to 180 degrees. So if you are going to purchase a square, go for an engineer's square with a dual protractor head and a square head.

SAWING

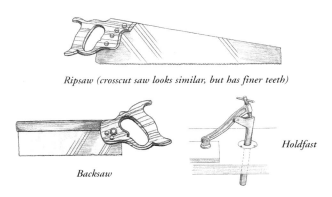

Ripsaw (crosscut saw looks similar, but has finer teeth)

Backsaw

Holdfast

Ripsaw, crosscut saw and backsaw

A ripsaw is designed to cut in the direction of the grain (down the length of a plank) while a crosscut saw is designed to cut at right angles to the run of the grain (across the width of a plank). If you intend to work with green slab wood, then you will need both saws. Once the wood has been sawn to size with the ripsaw and the crosscut saw, you will need to use one or other of the backsaws to make the finer cuts that are required for the project. We use a tenon saw for general bench work, and a gents saw for thin-section wood. Both these backsaws are used in conjunction with a traditional bench, vice, holdfast and/or portable patent trestle vice.

Bandsaw

The bandsaw is the perfect tool for cutting curves in thick-section wood. You can fit the saw with different sizes and grades of blade – a fine-toothed narrow blade for tight curves in thin-section wood, and a heavy-toothed wide blade for broader curves in thick-section wood. A small, two-wheeled bench-top

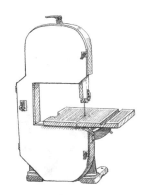

Bandsaw

machine is perfectly adequate for all the projects in this book. The wood is held down on the cutting table and manoeuvred so that the blade is presented with the line of cut. The primary safety rule is to always keep your fingers away from the front of the blade. If you have doubts, use a push-stick to advance the wood.

Scroll saw

While a bandsaw is used for cutting generous curves in thick-section wood, the scroll saw (sometimes called a jigsaw or fretsaw) is used for cutting intricate

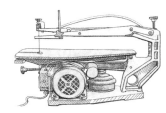

Scroll saw

curves in thin-section wood. The scroll saw is as safe as a machine can be. The very worst that you can do is scratch your fingers. The wood is held down firmly on the table and fed towards the jiggling blade. If you like fine, fretted curves, and you are working in a limited space, then the scroll saw is ideal.

Log saw

Hacksaw

Log saw and hacksaw

Generally, a log saw (sometimes called a bow saw) is not really considered to be a woodworking tool, but it is perfect for cutting damp, green barky wood. We use two very ordinary workaday saws – a large one for the rough task of cutting the wood into manageable lengths, and a smaller, easy-to-handle saw for little cuts. These saws can be purchased from DIY stores. You will also need a small hacksaw for cutting bolts and threaded rod.

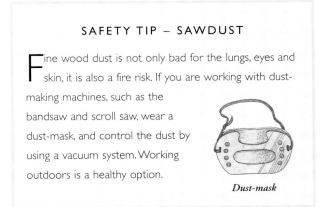

SAFETY TIP – SAWDUST

Fine wood dust is not only bad for the lungs, eyes and skin, it is also a fire risk. If you are working with dust-making machines, such as the bandsaw and scroll saw, wear a dust-mask, and control the dust by using a vacuum system. Working outdoors is a healthy option.

Dust-mask

CARVING

Gouge, mallet, adze, V-section tool and paring chisel

Gouges are designed to make a curved, scooping cut – appearing as a "U" or "C" in cross-section. The terms "straight", "bent", "curved" and "spoon" describe the shape of the blade along its length. Generally, straight gouges are used for surface work, while bent, curved and

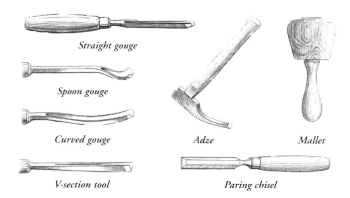

Straight gouge

Spoon gouge

Curved gouge

Adze

Mallet

V-section tool

Paring chisel

spoon gouges are used for scooping out holes. The piece of work is clamped to the bench – for this a sash clamp is ideal – and the gouge is used with or without a wooden mallet. The adze is used like an axe, and is good for carving hollows. The V-section tool cuts a furrow, while a paring chisel is designed to make skimming cuts.

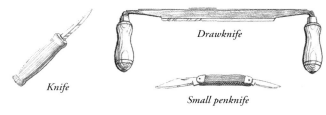

Drawknife

Knife

Small penknife

Knives and drawknives

A knife is a wonderful tool for all the trimming tasks involved in building bird houses and feeders. We use a small penknife for whittling pegs and for delicate shaping, and a larger knife for cutting rods and poles.

A drawknife is a two-handled knife that is used for tasks such as skinning poles and shaping rods. The workpiece is held secure in the vice or holdfast, while the drawknife is held in both hands and worked with a pulling, slicing stroke.

SAFETY TIP – KNIVES

Children tend to be fascinated by knives. Always keep knives in a locked cupboard and show the children how to use them when they are old enough.

DRILLING

Hand-held power drill

Clamp

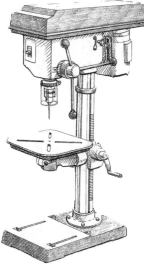

Bench drill press

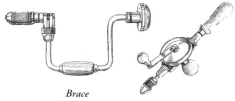

Brace

Pinion drill

Power drills

Ideally you should have two power-operated drills: a good-size bench drill press for large-diameter holes in component parts, and a hand-held drill for all the smaller holes that you need to make for nails, screws and bolts. If you do decide to use a hand-held power drill to bore large-diameter holes, you must secure the workpiece with clamps.

Hand drills

We have two hand drills: a traditional brace, and a small "egg beater-type" single-pinion drill. The brace is particularly useful for drilling deep, wide holes in unseasoned green wood, while the pinion drill is great for small-diameter holes in plywood and thin-section wood – when you can't be bothered to get out the electric drill.

Auger, twist and forstner bits

We use forstner bits in the drill press, a mix of forstner and twist bits in the electric drill, auger bits in the brace, and small twist bits in the pinion drill. Forstner bits are ideal for smooth-sided, flat-bottomed, large-diameter holes, and for getting rid of waste when carving.

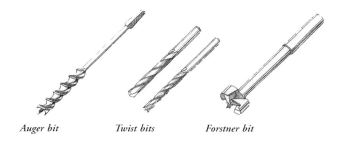

Auger bit   *Twist bits*   *Forstner bit*

ASSEMBLING

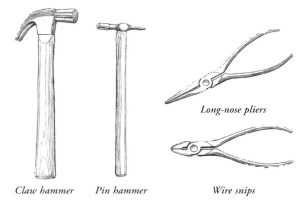

Long-nose pliers

Claw hammer   *Pin hammer*   *Wire snips*

Nails, panel pins, hammers and pliers

We favour using a mix of panel pins, steel nails and galvanized nails (see page 21): panel pins for thin-section wood and plywood, steel nails for thick-section green wood, and galvanized nails for just about everything else. You will need two hammers: a good-size claw hammer for driving in and drawing out large nails, and a pin hammer for knocking in small nails and pins accurately.

To assist nailing and to straighten and extract nails, you will need a pair of long-nose pliers; for cutting wire mesh, a pair of wire snips is required.

Screwdriver

Screws, screwdrivers and threaded rod

Screws (see page 21) and threaded rod (see page 20) are invaluable. We use screws rather than pins for fixing plywood when we require greater strength. Threaded rod is good for situations where you need bolts of a non-standard length: all you do is cut the threaded rod to length, and use it in conjunction with washers and nuts. Threaded rod comes in various lengths and diameters. You will need a range of screwdrivers to fit your chosen screws, and a hacksaw to cut the threaded rod to length.

Glue

Plywood is best fixed with glue and panel pins. We use exterior-grade PVA wood glue, which is tough and flexible, and as far as we know, does not give off vapours that are harmful to birds. Beware of two-mix glues, and glues that are petroleum based. It is a good idea to follow your nose – if a glue has a strong smell, birds will not like it.

SANDING AND PAINTING

Sandpaper and sanding blocks

Sanding is the technique of using graded abrasives to cut back a rough surface to a smooth finish. There are all manner of abrasives, but the projects in this book are best worked with a traditional sandpaper or glasspaper. The paper can either be folded (so that you can reach into tight corners) or it can be wrapped around a sanding block (in order to sand large, flat surfaces).

Sandpaper

Sanding block

Paints and finishes

We prefer to use water-based acrylics, applied in thin washes to enhance the character of the underlying wood. The wood must be rubbed down to a smooth finish before brushing on the paint. When it is dry, you can rub through the paint to achieve a distressed effect. Give the finished project a coat of water-based exterior matt or gloss varnish.

Paintbrush

MOUNTING METHODS

Bird houses and feeders need to be securely mounted on a tree, building, fence, wall or a freestanding pole. Look for a sheltered site (if on a building, make sure the bird house will not damage it), where the birds will be safe from predators. Ensure that the position does not present any hazards for birds or bird-watchers.

MOUNTING ON POLES

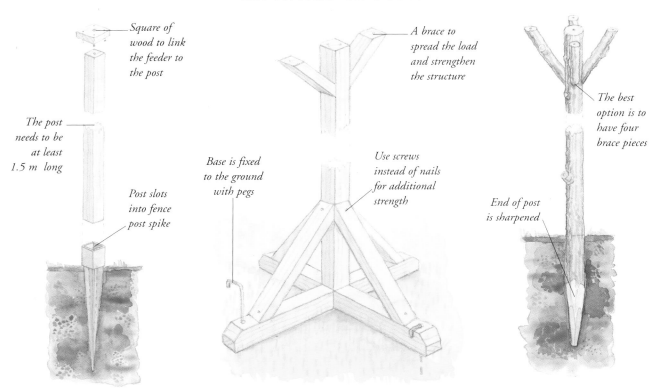

Square of wood to link the feeder to the post

The post needs to be at least 1.5 m long

Post slots into fence post spike

A brace to spread the load and strengthen the structure

Base is fixed to the ground with pegs

Use screws instead of nails for additional strength

The best option is to have four brace pieces

End of post is sharpened

Fence post with metal socket: *The socket is hammered into the ground, and the post is screwed or bolted into place.*

Freestanding bracket construction: *For additional support on a windy site, the stand is secured to the ground with tent pegs.*

Rustic post: *Quick to make and easy to replace, this design will blend into the fabric of the garden.*

Depending on the type and size of the bird house or feeder, it may be mounted on a freestanding pole. A pole can be banged or dug into the ground, slotted into a special metal fence post spike, or supported on its own bracketed base. The bracketed base gives you the option of easily repositioning the whole thing at a later date, but it does make for a lot more work. Banging the pole into the ground is perhaps the simplest method, but the bottom of the pole is likely to rot and decay. The metal fence spike will provide a stable structure, but you do have to consider buried electric cables, gas or water pipes. We prefer to hammer the pole straight into the ground – it's quick, and to our mind, the eventual rot and decay are all part and parcel of the natural "green" garden.

MOUNTING NESTBOXES ON BUILDINGS

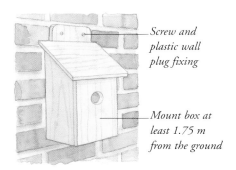

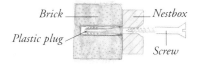

Fixing for concrete: *Use special bolts. Good for mounting heavy boxes (also for brick).*

Fixing for brick: *Use a screw and plug. Avoid fixing into the mortar coursing.*

Nestbox mounted on a brick wall: *For additional strength – and to stop the box tilting – use two fixings.*

Dovecote mounted on a wooden wall: *For heavy boxes, use metal fixing plates screwed to the back of the structure.*

Many birds favour boxes mounted on buildings – no doubt their bird sense tells them that buildings are, in many ways, akin to muddy banks, cliff faces and the like. You need to take into account what is best for the building, and what is best for the birds. The best type of fixing method is to use screws and rawlplugs, or small expanding bolts. It's much better to drill into the brick than the mortar, as it does less damage to the building, and is more secure for the box. Pick a spot that is away from windows, rainwater downpipes, tree branches and fences – you don't want rain dribbling into the box, or to allow cats and squirrels to reach the box by walking along a branch or fence. On no account drill holes into the sofit, as this is very often made of asbestos cement.

MOUNTING ON TREES

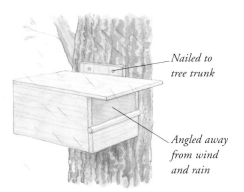

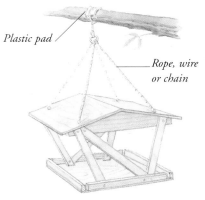

Mounting a chimney box: *Hang the box under a branch (facing upwards) to disguise it from predators.*

Mounting an open-front box: *Position the box so that the opening is sheltered from the worst of the weather.*

Mounting a hanging feeder: *The feeder is suspended from a substantial tree branch at a height that is easy to reach.*

Find a suitable mature tree, walk around it and try to work out which direction the prevailing weather comes from. Ideally, the box needs to be sited to face away from the wind and rain. Take into consideration the recommended box height for the birds you want to attract, and pick a spot that is safe from cats and squirrels. The box can be nailed, screwed or wired into place. Make sure it is stable, and avoid damaging the tree as much as possible. Some feeders can of course be suspended from a branch on a rope or wire.

Part 3

THE PROJECTS

Woodwork is a great activity in its own right – an exciting journey into the wonderful world of sawing, carving and drilling – and what better at the end of it all, than to have made a bird house or feeder? You and your family will be able to watch young birds being fed, tits getting up to their noisy antics – you will have created an engaging focal point in the garden. Even if you are more of a bird enthusiast than a woodworker, our carefully structured step-by-step projects will guide you to success.

NATURAL LOG TIT BOX

T*his log nesting box – sometimes known as the "Berlepsch" log box – is, without doubt, the greenest of tit boxes. Designed in the last quarter of the nineteenth century by the eccentric German landowner Baron Von Berlepsch, the whole idea of the box is to create (as near as possible) an exact replica of a natural nesting cavity. The design was first marketed by the RSPB (Royal Society for the Protection of Birds).*

DESIGN NOTES

The design is beautiful in its simplicity – just a hollowed-out log, a disc of wood for the base plug, a piece of plywood for the back board, a whittled peg and a few holes – and you have the ultimate in eco-friendly nest-boxes. If you like the notion of a tit box that will be at one with the trees, and if you enjoy basic woodcarving, then this is the project to make.

We selected a cherry log for the box – because it carves easily and looks good – but you can use any wood that takes your fancy, if it is reasonably straight-grained, easy to carve, and will blend in with the site.

Materials
- Cherry log, 380 mm long and about 200 mm in diameter (A)
- Exterior plywood, 380 mm long, 9 mm thick and 170 mm wide (B)
- Pine, 200 mm long, 45 mm thick and 200 mm wide (C)
- Pine, 230 mm long, 25 mm thick and 40 mm wide (D)
- Panel pins, 25 mm
- Nail for fixing, 80 mm

Tools
- Workbench with vice
- Pencil and ruler
- Small axe and chopping log
- Sash clamp
- Straight gouges, 12 mm and 25 mm wide
- Electric drill
- Bench drill press
- Forstner drill bits, 8 mm, 12 mm and 25 mm
- Bent gouge, 38 mm wide
- Mallet
- Pin and claw hammers
- Penknife

A BIRD-FRIENDLY BOX

M*any of our common garden birds nest in holes in trees, where eggs and chicks are safer from most common predators. With a shortage of suitable natural nest sites, this basic "tit box" is an essential feature of every bird-friendly garden.

The most likely occupants are Blue Tits or Great Tits, although depending on the location, House and Tree Sparrows, Nuthatches or even Pied Flycatchers may take advantage of a ready-made home.

Site your nestbox during autumn or winter, to allow the birds to get used to its presence. The best place is on a fence or wall facing from north-east to south-east, to avoid strong sunlight, and between 1.5 and 5 metres above the ground. It is also useful to try to tilt the front of the nestbox downwards a little, to create an overhang that will keep out the rain. The British Trust for Ornithology (see addresses on page 78), which organizes a National Nestbox Week every year, publishes a practical guide to nestboxes, which is available on request.

Once the birds have chosen to nest, there will be a period of frenetic activity, as they go to and fro with nesting material. Once egg-laying begins, things go quiet, though during incubation the male will bring food for the female. After hatching, the activity begins again, until a couple of weeks later the chicks finally leave the nest and face the outside world.*

Step 1: Axing the log

Step 2: Carving the roof slope

Step 3: Drilling out the waste

Step 4: Gouging the hollow

Step 5: Fitting the base plug

Step 6: Fitting the back board

Step 7: Drilling the access hole

Step 8: Whittling the peg

CONSTRUCTION DETAILS FOR THE NATURAL LOG TIT BOX

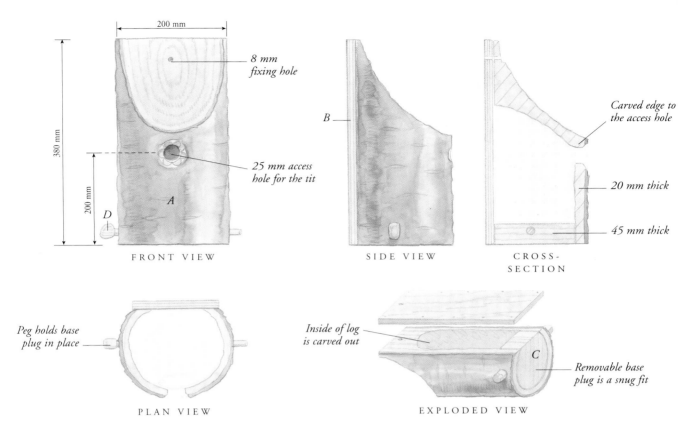

200 mm

8 mm
fixing hole

25 mm access
hole for the tit

380 mm

200 mm

A

D

FRONT VIEW

B

SIDE VIEW

Carved edge to
the access hole

20 mm thick

45 mm thick

CROSS-
SECTION

Peg holds base
plug in place

PLAN VIEW

Inside of log
is carved out

C

Removable base
plug is a snug fit

EXPLODED VIEW

HOW TO MAKE THE PROJECT

Step 1: Axing the log Having used a pencil and ruler to set out the length of the log (A), use the axe to work the back of the log to a flat finish about 170 mm wide.

Step 2: Carving the roof slope Support the end of the log against the sash clamp and use the straight gouges to carve the top of the log into a gentle slope.

Step 3: Drilling out the waste Set the log front face-down on the bench and use the drill and the 25 mm forstner bit to clear the bulk of the waste.

Step 4: Gouging the hollow Clamp the workpiece in the vice and use the bent gouge to scoop out the remaining waste. Aim for a hollow 165 mm in diameter.

Step 5: Fitting the base plug Trim the base plug (C) to snugly fit the hollow. Tap it into place with the mallet.

Step 6: Fitting the back board Cut the plywood board (B) to fit the back of the log and fix with the panel pins.

Step 7: Drilling the access hole Establish a hole centre 200 mm up from the base of the tit box, and use the 25 mm forstner drill bit (with the drill press) to bore the access hole through into the hollow.

Step 8: Whittling the peg Drill a hole 12 mm in diameter across the width of the log, through the wall thickness and through the base plug. Whittle a peg (D) for this hole. Drill an 8 mm hole at the top of the box.

MOUNTING

Select a suitable site on a fence, wall or stout tree, and position the box 1.5 to 5 metres above the ground. Angle the entrance hole away from strong sunlight and the prevailing winds, and nail the box firmly in place.

STANDARD OPEN-FRONT BOX

T*his traditional open-front design draws its inspiration from the type of Edwardian mailbox that was often hung in the porch of an English country house. Its fancy stepped profile, generous angled roof, and subtle colourwashed finish will enhance your garden. The carefully thought-out dimensions and structure of this box will attract birds such as Robins and flycatchers.*

DESIGN NOTES

If you have been looking for an open-front box for your garden, but you have been somewhat put off by the ill-considered, plywood-and-plastic bird houses that are usually on offer, then this project is tailor-made for you. The six-board design is wonderfully easy to make. All the boards are both glued and pinned – for extra strength and to keep out the weather – and the whole work is made from rough-sawn cherry, making it a choice project for the beginner who has a yen for something that little bit special.

Materials
- Cherry, 560 mm long, 17 mm thick and 200 mm wide (A)
- 2 x pieces cherry, 405 mm long, 17 mm thick and 137 mm wide (B)
- Cherry, 230 mm long, 17 mm thick and 196 mm wide (C)
- Cherry, 137 mm long, 17 mm thick and 166 mm wide (D)
- Cherry, 200 mm long, 17 mm thick and 95 mm wide (E)
- Exterior-grade PVA wood glue
- Panel pins, 40 mm
- Acrylic paint, pale green
- Clear exterior-quality varnish
- Screws, 2 x 50 mm

Tools
- Workbench with vice
- Pencil, ruler and compass
- Engineer's square
- Penknife
- Scroll saw fitted with a fine blade
- Electric drill
- Bench drill press
- Forstner drill bits, 10 mm and 25 mm
- Sandpaper and sanding block
- Pin hammer
- Small paintbrush
- Screwdriver

A VERSATILE BOX

S ome species of bird, including the Robin, Pied Wagtail and Spotted Flycatcher, prefer to make a nest in a crevice, or build a cup-shaped nest in a suitable nook or cranny. For them, the best nestbox design is one with an open front.

The nice thing about this design is that you don't have to be too accurate with your measurements – after all, natural crevices aren't always perfectly shaped! Another advantage is that you can easily inspect the box and its contents, enabling you to see the eggs and chicks – but don't spend too long looking, or you might cause the birds to desert.

The only drawback is that this kind of nestbox leaves the occupants very vulnerable to predation, especially from Jays, Magpies and cats.

As with the tit box, choose a sheltered site, where the birds are protected from prevailing wind, rain and direct sunlight. Placing the box amongst some foliage – for example a climbing plant such as a clematis, can provide shelter and some protection against intruders. Also, keep the box away from bird tables and feeders as the presence of feeding birds nearby may deter potential occupants from nesting.

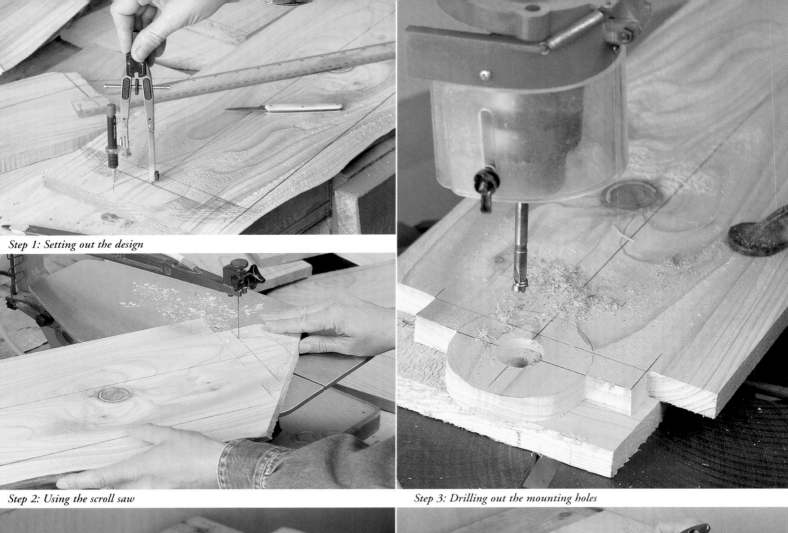

Step 1: Setting out the design

Step 2: Using the scroll saw

Step 3: Drilling out the mounting holes

Step 4: Fitting together

Step 5: Applying the colourwash

Step 6: Rubbing down and finishing

CONSTRUCTION DETAILS FOR THE OPEN-FRONT BOX

196 mm

110 mm

CROSS-SECTION

200 mm

25 mm

37.5 mm

15 mm

95 mm

100 mm

20 mm

37.5 mm radius

FRONT VIEW

77.5 mm

560 mm

57.5 mm

SIDE VIEW

25 mm and 10 mm holes

C

A

D

B

E

EXPLODED VIEW

PLAN VIEW

HOW TO MAKE THE PROJECT

Step 1: Setting out the design Set out the back board (A) with the ruler and engineer's square. To mark out the decorative half-circle on both ends, fix the compass to a radius of 37.5 mm, spike the point on the centre-line, 37.5 mm in from the end of the board, and draw the half-circle. Mark out the steps with the penknife.

Step 2: Using the scroll saw Cut out the half-circle and steps on the back board (A). Cut out the other pieces (B, C, D and E). Advance the workpiece at a steady pace, with the cutting line slightly to the waste side of the drawn line.

Step 3: Drilling out the mounting holes Using the 25 mm forstner bit and the drill press, drill to a depth of about 8 mm – half the thickness of the back board (A). Change to the 10 mm bit and continue to drill right through the board. Do this on both ends of the board.

Step 4: Fitting together Sand down the edges of all the pieces to a smooth, square finish. Apply the glue to all mating faces, and join. Fix with the panel pins.

Step 5: Applying the colourwash Dilute the acrylic paint with water and brush on repeated washes until you have an attractive density of colour.

Step 6: Rubbing down and finishing Use the sandpaper to rub away areas of the paint to reveal the grain and create a worn appearance. Varnish.

MOUNTING

Spend time selecting a suitable site about 1.5 to 5 metres above the ground – it might be on a wooden shed, a wall, or a limb or fork of a stout tree. Position the box to face away from the prevailing wind and rain, and screw it firmly in place.

BARK TREECREEPER BOX

T*he Treecreeper box is a winner on many counts. The bark is left intact so that the box is perfectly camouflaged; it is made from easy-to-work green wood; the interior surfaces are rough-sawn and gouge-textured, providing good footholds for the nestlings; and the whole project can be assembled easily and quickly.*

DESIGN NOTES

The clever thing about this design is the way the back slab is cut and worked, so that the front and roof slabs notch together allowing the rain to run down and off the box without entering it. The bark on the front of the box runs from top to bottom, making it almost invisible when it is mounted on a tree. Perhaps most importantly of all, in view of the concerns about declining wood resources, the design uses first-cut sawmill wood that would otherwise be wasted.

When you are searching for wood, do your best to select sound slabs of hardwood with the bark still firmly attached. If the wood is in any way faulted – long splits, spongy areas, pierced with large insect holes – then look around for another piece.

Materials

(All thickness measurements are necessarily average, with some slabs being considerably thicker in part.)

- Sawn oak, 600 mm long, 36 mm thick and 160 mm wide (A)
- Sawn oak, 270 mm long, 25 mm thick and 210 mm wide (B)
- 2 x pieces sawn oak, 270 mm long, 25 mm thick and 150 mm wide (C)
- Sawn oak, 189 mm long, 25 mm thick and 240 mm wide (D)
- Galvanized nails, 50 mm
- 2 x galvanized nails, 80 mm

Tools

- Workbench with vice
- Pencil, ruler, square and dividers
- Small bandsaw
- Small log saw
- Straight gouge, 30 mm wide
- Mallet
- Pin and claw hammers

TREECREEPER HOME

T*he* Treecreeper is one of our most endearing little birds, and also one of the easiest to overlook. As the name suggests, Treecreepers spend most of their lives creeping up tree trunks, and along branches, in search of food – tiny insects and spiders – which they prise from beneath the bark with their narrow, decurved bill. Their dull brown plumage and creeping habit make this bird difficult to see.

Treecreepers are one of the most sedentary of birds, and are highly vulnerable during prolonged spells of icy weather, especially when "glazed frosts" cover twigs and branches with a thin layer of ice.

They are woodland birds, so are not frequent visitors to most gardens. However, if you have a large garden in the country it is well worth considering the intriguing design of this nestbox. You could also erect the box in nearby woodland, provided that you obtain permission from the owner first.

The idea of this box is to make it look as much like the natural nesting site of the Treecreeper as possible. Treecreepers generally nest in tiny cracks and crevices beneath the bark, using twigs, stems, roots and bark – the nest is often concealed behind a curtain of ivy. They usually lay five or six pale, slightly spotted eggs.

As with all nestboxes, take special care when siting the Treecreeper box, as a fall from a tree can be dangerous. Use a sturdy ladder and ask a partner to hold it steady while you fix the box.

Step 1: Setting out the wood

Step 2: Using the bandsaw

Step 3: Using the log saw

Step 4: Cutting the back board notches

Step 5: Fitting the side boards

Step 6: Putting together

CONSTRUCTION DETAILS FOR THE BARK TREECREEPER BOX

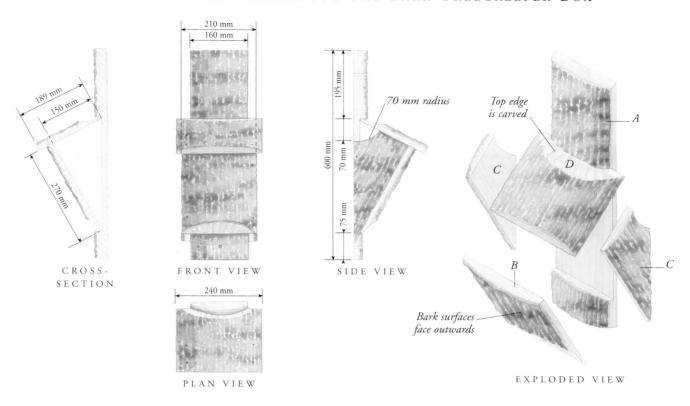

210 mm
160 mm

189 mm
150 mm
270 mm

195 mm
600 mm
70 mm
75 mm

70 mm radius

Top edge
is carved

A

C
D

B

C

Bark surfaces
face outwards

CROSS-
SECTION

FRONT VIEW

SIDE VIEW

EXPLODED VIEW

240 mm

PLAN VIEW

HOW TO MAKE THE PROJECT

Step 1: Setting out the wood Use the pencil, ruler, square and dividers to set out the measurements on the sawn face of the wood. Do your best to avoid deep knot-holes, twisted grain and splits.

Step 2: Using the bandsaw Cut out the pieces. Bearing in mind that you will have to cut the wood with the bark face on the underside (consequently the blade will snatch), you must be extra careful to keep your fingers well away from the front of the blade. You will need help with the larger boards.

Step 3: Using the log saw Run the two stop-cut notches halfway through the 36 mm thickness of the back board (A). Aim to finish up with the bottom of the cuts parallel to the back sawn face of the wood.

Step 4: Cutting the back board notches Use the mallet and gouge to remove the waste between the two stop-cut notches. Hold the gouge at a low angle and work from centre through to end – so that the length of the gouge stroke is controlled by the stop-cut. Clear the waste from one end, then turn the wood around and repeat the procedure for the other end.

Step 5: Fitting the side boards Have a trial dry-run so that you know how the project comes together, and then nail the two side boards (C) firmly in place on the back board, using the pin hammer and the 50 mm nails.

Step 6: Putting together When you are satisfied with the stability and appearance of the structure, go over the whole box, fixing with additional nails.

MOUNTING

Choose a suitable tree, and position the box about 2.5 to 5 metres above the ground, with the side entrance holes in a sheltered spot away from strong sunlight. Using the claw hammer, fix firmly in place with the 80 mm nails at top and bottom.

TAWNY OWL CHIMNEY BOX

For many bird lovers, the very thought of having owls in the garden tops the excitement scale. For the chance to watch owls swooping to rest, "twit-twooing" to each other, the mother owl bringing food for her young and chicks learning to fly, – this box is a must-have!

DESIGN NOTES

In many ways, this design is delightful in its simplicity – not much more than five in-bark slabs nailed together to make a box. But fresh-sawn green wood is damp, difficult to saw up, subject to faults, and heavy. The best way to deal with it is to use large-toothed saws and oil the blades, to pre-drill nail holes, and to get help with lifting.

As green wood tends to be cheap, you can even make a mock-up version first, to iron out potential problems. If you are a fan of large-scale, instant-result woodwork, you will enjoy this project.

Materials

(All thickness measurements are necessarily average, with some slabs being considerably thicker in part.)

- Sawn oak, 820 mm long, 60 mm thick and 280 mm wide (A)
- 2 x pieces sawn oak, 680 mm long, 56 mm thick and 164 mm wide (B)
- Sawn oak, 680 mm long, 56 mm thick and 208 mm wide (C)
- Sawn oak, 164 mm long, 60 mm thick and 164 mm wide (D)
- Vegetable oil
- Galvanized nails, 80 mm
- Galvanized wire

Tools

- Workbench with vice, holdfast and bench stop
- Pencil, ruler, straight-edge and square
- Ripsaw
- Log saw
- Straight gouge, 25 mm wide
- Mallet
- Electric drill
- Twist drill bit, 5 mm
- Claw hammer

HUNTERS IN YOUR GARDEN

The hooting call of the Tawny Owl is surely one of the most familiar sounds of the countryside, yet the bird itself is rarely seen, due to its predominantly nocturnal lifestyle. Occasionally, a Tawny Owl may be discovered at a daytime roost, where it can allow a very close approach.

Nestboxes come in all sorts of shapes and sizes, each designed to attract a particular species, or group of species. As hole nesters, Tawny Owls can be enticed to use nestboxes with this specially-designed "chimney box". Made to resemble a hollowed-out piece of wood, it should be attached firmly to the underside of a sturdy branch, using wire or straps.

Tawny Owls are highly sedentary, spending most of their lives in a very small area, even during the harsh winter weather. They are most often found in gardens near mixed or deciduous woodland, or those with plenty of mature trees in which the owls can breed and roost and where they hunt their rodent prey.

Owls are early nesters, so make sure you put the box up in autumn or early winter. Ideally you should check to make sure there are owls in the local area first, which will maximize your chances of success. Tawny Owls lay between two and five white eggs, which they incubate for four weeks. The young often leave the nest before they are fully fledged.

Step 1: Setting out the slabs

Step 2: Cutting the wood

Step 3: Using the gouge

Step 4: Dry-run put-together

Step 5: Drilling the nail holes

Step 6: Putting together

CONSTRUCTION DETAILS FOR THE TAWNY OWL CHIMNEY BOX

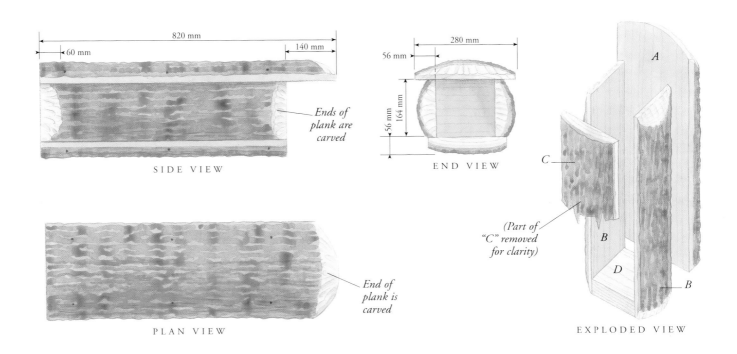

820 mm

60 mm

140 mm

Ends of plank are carved

SIDE VIEW

280 mm

56 mm

164 mm

56 mm

END VIEW

A

C

(Part of "C" removed for clarity)

B

D

B

EXPLODED VIEW

End of plank is carved

PLAN VIEW

HOW TO MAKE THE PROJECT

Step 1: Setting out the slabs Check your chosen wood for potential problems such as dead knots, splits and spongy areas, and avoid them. Use the pencil, ruler, straight-edge and square to set out all the measurements on the sawn face of the wood.

Step 2: Cutting the wood Clamp the wood firmly in the vice, bridging it across the open vice, with the holdfast clamping down the tail end of the slab. Wipe a small amount of vegetable oil over the blade of the ripsaw – to keep the blade moving freely and to stop it rusting – and cut out the pieces. Use the log saw to cut the leading end of the roof slab (A) to a rounded finish.

Step 3: Using the gouge Butt the end of the workpiece hard up against a bench stop (a piece of plywood nailed to the bench) and use the mallet and gouge to cut the end of the wood to a gently sloped finish. Do this on the leading end of the roof slab (A), and on both ends of the side slabs (B). Leave the gouge marks showing.

Step 4: Dry-run put-together Support the base slab (C) in the vice and establish the position of the two side slabs (B) and the end piece (D). Mark out registration lines so that you know precisely how the wood comes together.

Step 5: Drilling the nail holes With the twist drill bit, drill holes for the nails to prevent the wood from splitting. Do this on the base slab (C) and the roof slab (A).

Step 6: Putting together Use the claw hammer to nail the base slab (C) to both side slabs (B) and the end piece (D), then turn the whole work over and nail the roof slab in place. The nails must not protrude inside the box.

MOUNTING

Find a good-size branch (one that is angled upwards from the trunk) at a point about 5 metres up the tree. Position the box with its entrance out of direct sunlight and with some shelter from the elements, and then secure it with three or more straps of galvanized wire.

JAPANESE BIRD BATH

This project draws its inspiration from the wonderful, calming imagery of traditional Japanese Zen gardens. The monolithic block of wood mounted on the tree stump takes on much the same role as the Japanese sentinel or guardian stone, the carved ripples on the surface of the wood symbolize waves, and the attractive hollow filled with water makes a perfect bird bath – all beautiful!

DESIGN NOTES

While in many ways this is the simplest of projects – not much more than a slab of wood with a carved hollow – the actual size and weight of the wood does make for difficulties. On the other hand, the wood is so heavy that it doesn't need to be held or clamped. We found that the best way of working was simply to set the slab on the ground (under cover), and then to move around it. As for the choice of wood, it is vital to pick an easy-to-carve hardwood. We chose a slab of straight-grained, knot-free English lime. When you are selecting the slab of wood, make sure that it is well seasoned – meaning that the wood has been allowed to dry for at least a year. Lime is particularly suited to this project as it is relatively easy to acquire and simple to carve – it is generally a wood that can't be bettered. This is an especially good project for those new to woodcarving.

Materials
- Lime slab, 764 mm long, 150 mm thick and 588 mm wide (A)
- Tree section, about 460 mm long and 400 mm in diameter (B)

Tools
- Pencil, ruler, straight-edge and felt-tip marker
- Tracing paper, 764 mm long and 588 mm wide
- Electric drill
- Forstner drill bits, 25 mm and 50 mm
- Adze
- Wooden mallets, heavyweight and lightweight
- Straight gouges, 25 mm and 40 mm
- Bent gouge, 25 mm
- V-section tool

BATH TIME FOR BIRDS

A well-made bird bath is one of the essential ingredients in creating a truly bird-friendly garden, giving the birds a regular source of clean water to drink and bathe in. This design is practical and sturdy, as well as being a very attractive piece of garden furniture.

Birds come in all shapes and sizes, so a bird bath needs to have a "shallow end" and a "deep end". Keep the bath filled on a daily basis, perhaps more frequently in hot weather. Every week or so, give your bird bath a thorough clean (you can use household cleaners, but rinse the bath thoroughly afterwards to remove any trace of chemicals). In harsh winter weather, make sure the water doesn't freeze by topping it up with warm water from time to time.

Most birds bathe at least once a day, generally in the morning or evening. Bathing is vital for birds to keep their plumage clean and their feathers in tip-top condition. It is especially important in winter, as it allows them to fluff out their feathers properly to insulate themselves against the cold. As natural sources of water such as lakes and ponds may be some distance away, many garden birds depend on those provided by us, either in the form of bird baths or garden ponds.

Ideally your bird bath should be sited in an open area, to minimize the chances of cats sneaking up on the birds as they wash or drink.

Step 1: Setting out the design

Step 2: Drilling out the waste

Step 3: Roughing out with the adze and gouge

Step 4: Hollowing out

Step 5: Cutting the V-grooves

CONSTRUCTION DETAILS FOR THE JAPANESE BIRD BATH

764 mm

184 mm

96 mm

70 mm grid

76 mm

588 mm

128 mm

PLAN VIEW

150 mm

48 mm

CROSS-SECTION

B (460 mm long, 400 mm in diameter)

DETAIL

HOW TO MAKE THE PROJECT

Step 1: Setting out the design Trace out the design at full size. With a pencil, press-transfer the traced lines through to the face of the wood (A). Establish the centre of the hollow and use the straight-edge and felt-tip marker to rule lines that radiate out from the centre.

Step 2: Drilling out the waste Remember that the hollow needs to be deepest at the narrow end. Use the drill to clear the bulk of the waste. Start with the larger forstner bit for boring out the widest and deepest holes, and then follow up with the smaller bit.

Step 3: Roughing out with the adze and gouge Use the adze to cut down to the depth of the drilled holes. Hold the adze at a fairly flat angle, and work from the drawn line through to the centre. Be careful not to sink the blade too deeply. With the mallets and the 40 mm straight gouge, tidy up the deepest part of the hollow.

Step 4: Hollowing out Use the 25 mm straight gouge to establish the edge of the hollow – you need a nice, clean smooth curve – and skim the surface to a smooth finish with the bent gouge. Work with smaller and smaller strokes until you achieve a fine, ripple-textured finish.

Step 5: Cutting the V-grooves Hold the V-section tool at a low angle and work from the edge of the hollow towards the edge of the wood. Be very careful not to dig too deeply into the wood. Continue until the pattern of grooves completely covers the surface of the wood.

MOUNTING

When you have selected a suitable site – preferably within view of your house and well away from prowling cats and noisy children – set the tree stump (B) in place, check that it is firm and level, and then get help to lift the slab into position.

BRAIN-TEASER FEEDER

*T*he whole idea of the brain-teaser feeder is that it allows small birds to comfortably eat their fill, while preventing big birds or pests such as squirrels from getting a look-in. The small birds can just about squeeze between the wooden dowels, and then on through the wire mesh to the peanuts that are contained in the mesh core.

DESIGN NOTES

The brain-teaser feeder is made up of seven primary elements. There is a large green disc roof that doubles up as a lid, two smaller yellow discs and a ring of wooden dowels that form the outer cage or first barrier, an inner wall of wire mesh that forms the second barrier, and a central mesh cage to hold the nuts. The whole work is held together with a twist of galvanized wire.

To fill the central cage with nuts, you simply slide the green disc up the wire, and trickle the nuts through the hole at the centre of the topmost yellow disc. If you like working with a compass, and are adept with a scroll saw, this project will keep you absorbed. When you come to mount the project in the garden, you have to bear in mind that while the feeder must be within reach, it also needs to be away from predators.

Materials

- Exterior plywood, disc 305 mm in diameter and 5.5 mm thick (A)
- Exterior plywood, 2 x discs 200 mm in diameter and 9 mm thick (B) (C)
- Doweling, 12 x lengths of 200 mm, 9 mm in diameter (D)
- Exterior plywood, disc 60 mm in diameter and 9 mm thick (E)
- Exterior plywood, disc 92 mm in diameter and 9 mm thick (F)
- Exterior plywood, disc 40 mm in diameter and 9 mm thick (G)
- Wire mesh, 350 mm long, 160 mm wide and 25 x 25 mm grid (H)
- Wire mesh, 180 mm long, 160 mm wide, 6 x 6 mm grid (I)
- Exterior-grade PVA wood glue
- Panel pins, 12 mm and 25 mm
- Acrylic paint, green and yellow
- Matt exterior-quality varnish
- Galvanized wire, 4 x lengths of 550 mm (J)

Tools

- Workbench with vice
- Pencil, ruler, square and compass
- Scroll saw
- Electric drill
- Bench drill press
- Forstner drill bits, 2 mm, 9 mm and 40 mm
- Long-nose pliers, wire snips
- Pin hammer
- Sandpaper and sanding block
- Paintbrush, 20 mm

BAN UNWELCOME GUESTS

*T*here's nothing more annoying than putting out expensive, high-quality food for the birds, only to watch it being eaten by squirrels – especially if they destroy the feeder in the process. So why not try making a feeder which lets the birds in – while keeping the squirrels out?

The design is simple but effective: thin dowel rods allow small birds such as sparrows, finches and even – at a squeeze – Starlings, to reach the food. As a bonus, this feeder also acts as a partial deterrent to cats, which find it hard to reach the feeding birds.

The only potential drawback is that some birds, particularly shyer species, may be wary of entering the bars at first. However, once they get used to it you should find that the birds soon take advantage of a squirrel-proof food supply – and you save money! The only losers are the squirrels, who hopefully will head off for easier pickings in a neighbour's garden.

Step 1: Setting out the discs

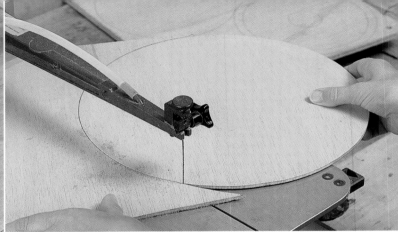

Step 2: Sawing the discs

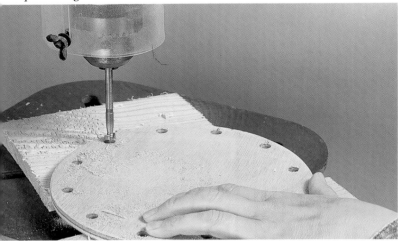

Step 3: Drilling the dowel holes

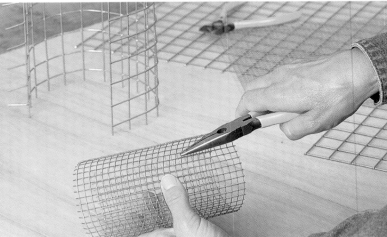

Step 4: Cutting and shaping the wire mesh

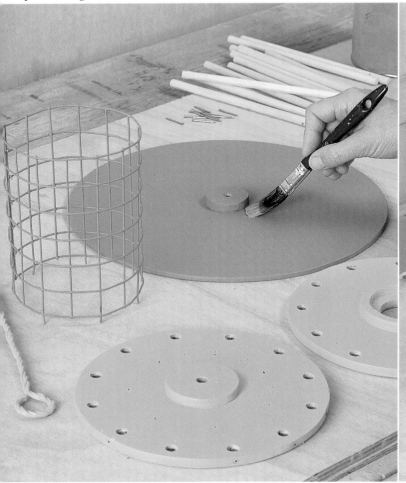

Step 5: Gluing and painting

Step 6: Fitting together

CONSTRUCTION DETAILS FOR THE BRAIN-TEASER FEEDER

90 mm

200 mm

160 mm

31 mm

200 mm diameter, 9 mm thick

9 mm dowel, 200 mm long

FRONT VIEW

305 mm diameter, 5.5 mm thick

PLAN VIEW

200 mm diameter, 9 mm thick

UNDERSIDE DETAIL

G *(under A)*

A

B

F *(with 64 mm diameter hole sawn into it)*

I

D

H

hole for wire

hole for dowel

C

E

J

EXPLODED VIEW

HOW TO MAKE THE PROJECT

Step 1: Setting out the discs Use the compass to set out the green lid (A), the plug (G), the two yellow discs (B and C), the peanut cage bottom disk (E), and the disc-ring (F) for over the top of the peanut cage.

Step 2: Sawing the discs Having drawn out the six discs, carefully cut them out with the scroll saw. Work at a steady pace in order to achieve clean, smooth curves.

Step 3: Drilling the dowel holes Sandwich the two 200 mm discs (B and C), set out the position of the 12 dowel holes and, using the drill press, drill them with the 9 mm forstner bit. Separate the discs and then use the 40 mm bit to run a hole through one of the discs.

Step 4: Cutting and shaping the wire mesh To make the outer cage (H) and the peanut cage (I), cut the wire mesh to size with the wire snips. Leave extra "fingers" of wire on one mating edge. Bend the mesh into shape and fold the fingers around the other edge with the pliers.

Step 5: Gluing and painting Glue the three small discs (E, F and G) in place and fix with 12 mm pins. Drill 9 mm holes through the centres of the lid and base. Smooth all surfaces with sandpaper. Apply a coat of acrylic paint. When dry, coat them with matt varnish. Make up the central rod (J) from a twist of four wires.

Step 6: Fitting together Slide the dowels (D) in place and fix with the 25 mm panel pins. Drill a ring of holes for the outer cage with the 2 mm drill bit. Sit the "fingers" of the cage in the holes. Locate the peanut cage in the holding ring and slide it into position. Fit the green lid, slide the twisted central holding rod through the whole work, and loop the ends to secure it.

MOUNTING

Select a sheltered site, such as under a tree or house eaves, and position the feeder at a height that is comfortable to reach. Hang it up with wire or strong twine. Finally, fill the inner cage with nuts, and wait for your first visitors.

RUSTIC BIRD FEEDER

This project has been fired by childhood memories. When I was about eight, I dreamt of being a trapper-cum-wild man like Robin Hood or Davy Crockett. Armed only with a penknife, I used to roam through the woods making bows and arrows and fishing rods. The Rustic Bird Feeder has been inspired by these memories. (ALAN)

DESIGN NOTES

This design uses green coppice wood (obtained from a woodsman who supplies round-section fence posts, logs, garden poles and the like), so all the diameter measurements are a very general guide. You will have to purchase the nearest available size, and then whittle and trim back to the given dimensions. Part of the joy of working with green wood is that every single stick and pole is unique.

FEEDING HABITS

From a bird's point of view, the bird table is the centrepiece of your garden. It enables you to provide a wide variety of different foods, suitable for many different kinds of birds which feed at different levels. Perching birds such as sparrows and Starlings will feed on the solid base, while you can hang extra feeders for tits and finches. Meanwhile, ground-feeding birds such as pigeons, doves, thrushes and Blackbirds will feed on spilled food beneath the table.

On a cautionary note, a badly sited bird table may enable cats or Sparrowhawks to help themselves to an easy meal by snatching one of the feeding birds. It is best to site your table a little away from nearby trees, bushes or fence posts, though not so far that the birds can't use them as cover to approach.

Always keep your bird table well stocked, and make sure you clear up any uneaten food every couple of days, as well as giving the new table a good scrub with soap and water every month or so.

Materials

- 4 x ash poles, 1750 mm long and 35–40 mm in diameter (A)
- 4 x ash poles, 650 mm long and 35–40 mm in diameter (B)
- 4 x ash poles, 425 mm long and 35–40 mm in diameter (C)
- Rough-sawn oak board, 475 mm long, 25 mm thick and 400 mm wide (D)
- 2 x sawn oak rods, 475 mm long, 20 mm thick and 20 mm wide (E)
- 2 x sawn oak rods, 360 mm long, 20 mm thick and 20 mm wide (F)
- Ash stick, 600 mm long, 25–35 mm in diameter (G)
- 2 x sawn oak boards, 425 mm long, 20 mm thick and 275 mm wide (H)
- 6 x sawn pine slats, 435 mm long, 5 mm thick and 150 mm wide (I)
- 4 x cut pegs, 150 mm long and 25 mm in diameter (J)
- 4 x cut pegs, 125 mm long and 25 mm in diameter (K)
- 2 x sawn oak boards, 435 mm long, 20 mm thick and 250 mm wide (L)
- 4 x cut pegs, 160 mm long, 25 mm in diameter (M)
- 2 x sawn oak rods, 435 mm long, 20 mm thick and 20 mm wide (N)
- 4 x cut pegs, 120 mm long, 25 mm in diameter (O)
- Panel pins, 25 mm and 40 mm
- Strong twine

Tools

- Workbench with vice and holdfast
- Pencil, ruler, square and compass
- Sash clamp
- Drawknife
- Penknife
- Brace
- Auger bits, 10 mm and 30 mm
- Crosscut saw
- Pin hammer

Step 1: Using the drawknife

Step 2: Boring out the peg holes

Step 3: Nailing the roof boards

Step 4: Making the food table

Step 5: Fixing the roof in place

Step 6: Finishing

CONSTRUCTION DETAILS FOR THE RUSTIC BIRD FEEDER

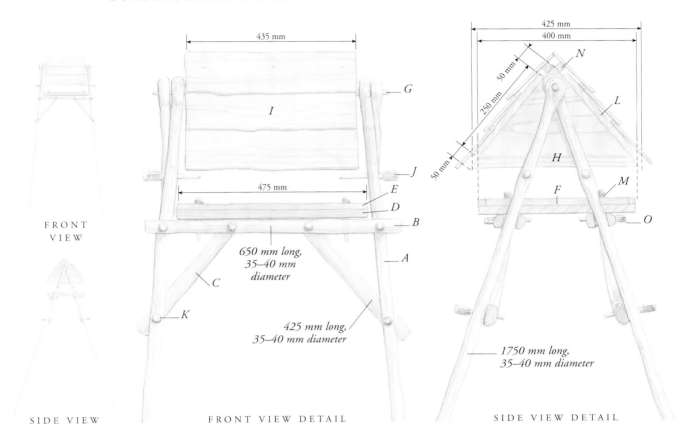

FRONT VIEW

435 mm

I

G

J

475 mm

E

D

B

*650 mm long,
35–40 mm
diameter*

C

A

K

*425 mm long,
35–40 mm diameter*

425 mm

400 mm

N

50 mm

250 mm

L

50 mm

H

F

M

O

*1750 mm long,
35–40 mm diameter*

SIDE VIEW

FRONT VIEW DETAIL

SIDE VIEW DETAIL

HOW TO MAKE THE PROJECT

Step 1: Using the drawknife Use the pencil, square and compass to set out the components. Put the poles in the vice and bridge them across the sash clamp. Hold the drawknife with the bevel on the underside (to control the depth of the cut) and trim the poles to size. Rerun this procedure for all the large round sections. Use the penknife to whittle all the pegs to shape.

Step 2: Boring out the peg holes Use the brace and the appropriate auger bit to bore out the holes – 10 mm for the pegs, and 30 mm for the two roof-board holes. Use the bench holdfast to secure the difficult-to-hold shapes.

Step 3: Nailing the roof boards Cut the roof triangles (H) to shape with the crosscut saw and nail the roof boards and slats (I) in place. Overlap the slats by 40 mm and pin the top slats to the oak rods (N). Use as many of the 25 mm and 40 mm panel pins as necessary.

Step 4: Making the food table Use the 40 mm panel pins to nail the 20 mm-square rods (E and F) around the top edge of the sawn oak board (D) to make a 20 mm-deep tray. Drive the panel pins in from both sides – down through the rods, and up through the board.

Step 5: Fixing the roof in place Fix the basic frame of the structure together with the wooden pegs and push the ridge stick (G) into position through the roof.

Step 6: Finishing Slide the tray in place – so that the pegs (M) slot down between the supporting horizontal cross-poles (B). Finally, lash the joints with strong twine.

MOUNTING

Select a site in view of the house, make sure that the main poles are well spread and secure, put some food scraps on the tray, and then sit back and enjoy the action.

FEEDING STATION

T*he feeding station is reminiscent of Pennsylvanian German barns – lots of arched windows, steep roofs and colour. With bunkers jam-packed full of peanuts, and with a bar for hanging lumps of lard and the like, it is a paradise for birds.*

DESIGN NOTES

The clever thing about this design is that in bad weather, the birds can go inside and feed in comfort.

The scroll-sawing procedure has been simplified, with the dimensions sized so that the sawing can be achieved without the need to drill pilot holes. All you do is saw from the bottom edge straight up the door-window centre-line, cutting away the waste in two halves.

Materials

- 2 x pieces exterior plywood, 470 mm long, 9 mm thick and 484 mm wide (A)
- 2 x pieces exterior plywood, 354 mm long, 5 mm thick and 120 mm wide (B)
- 2 x pieces exterior plywood, 354 mm long, 5 mm thick and 140 mm wide (C)
- 2 x pieces exterior plywood, 354 mm long, 5 mm thick and 132 mm wide (D)
- 2 x pieces exterior plywood, 312 mm long, 9 mm thick and 100 mm wide (E)
- 2 x pieces exterior plywood, 312 mm long, 9 mm thick and 80 mm wide (F)
- 2 x pieces exterior plywood, 312 mm long, 9 mm thick and 80 mm wide (G)
- Exterior plywood, 708 mm long, 9 mm thick and 604 mm wide (H)
- Pine, 1416 mm long, 20 x 20 mm square section (I)
- Pine, 1208 mm long, 20 x 20 mm square section (J)
- Exterior plywood, 312 mm long, 9 mm thick and 466 mm wide (K)
- Exterior plywood, 312 mm long, 9 mm thick and 298 mm wide (L)
- Exterior plywood 708 mm long, 5 mm thick and 10 mm wide (M)
- Doweling, 500 mm long, 15 mm in diameter (N)
- Wire mesh, 500 mm long, 500 mm wide (this allows for cutting waste), 6 x 6 mm grid (O)
- 2 x rustic fence posts, 2 metres long and 70 mm in diameter (P)
- 6 x steel flap hinges, 40 mm long and 35 mm wide
- Steel countersunk screws to fit the hinges, 5 mm
- Nails, 80 mm
- Panel pins, 12 mm and 20 mm
- Staples, 5 mm
- Exterior-grade PVA wood glue
- Acrylic paint, brick red and blue
- Clear exterior-quality varnish

Tools

- Workbench with vice
- Pencil, ruler, engineer's square and compass
- Scroll saw
- Electric drill
- Bench drill press
- Forstner drill bit, 40 mm
- Screwdriver
- Long-nose pliers
- Pin and claw hammers
- Paintbrush, 25 mm
- Sandpaper and sanding block

BIRD NOTES

If you want to provide a real gourmet service for your garden birds, why not make a full-scale feeding station. This is a high-class bird table, with different areas for different kinds of food, including seeds, fruit and scraps.

As with bird tables, it is essential that you site your feeding station in the right place. Keep it well-stocked, clear away spilt or uneaten food, and clean it regularly.

Keep a log of which birds use it, how often, and for how long. Also, watch out for unusual visitors, especially in winter, when harsh weather often forces birds from the surrounding countryside to venture into gardens in search of food. Look out for Coal and Marsh Tits, Nuthatches, Blackcaps, Great Spotted Woodpeckers and our two winter thrushes, Redwings and Fieldfares.

Step 1: Setting out the plywood

Step 2: Scroll-sawing the door-windows

Step 3: Nailing the walls together

Step 4: Painting and fitting

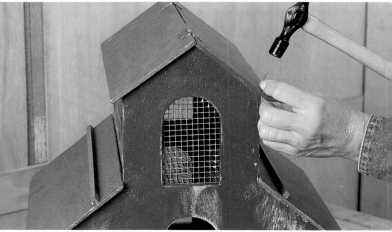

Step 5: Fixing the wire mesh

Step 6: Fixing the roof

CONSTRUCTION DETAILS FOR THE FEEDING STATION

112 mm
100 mm
60 mm
60 mm
50 mm
92 mm
O
30 mm radius
A
38 mm
40 mm hole
9 mm
thick
708 mm
P
N
J
L
K
I
H
Drainage hole

354 mm
312 mm
40.5 mm
12 mm
77 mm | 77 mm | 77 mm
470 mm
B
60 mm
40 mm
*50 mm
40 mm
hole
E
80 mm
20 mm
C
M
*40 mm
F
D
*40 mm
G
9 mm thick
20 x 20 mm
section
604 mm

SIDE VIEW

*Position of centre-line from
bottom edge of component*

FRONT VIEW

(hinges fitted
40 mm from
outside edge)

EXPLODED VIEW

HOW TO MAKE THE PROJECT

Step 1: Setting out the plywood Use the pencil, ruler, square and compass to set out the design on the plywood. Make the gable ends (A) identical and draw centre-lines up through the door-windows.

Step 2: Scroll-sawing the door-windows Run the saw cut straight in from the bottom edge of the wood and up the centre-line. Manoeuvre the wood so as to work to the waste side of the drawn line, and exit along the same cut.

Step 3: Nailing the walls together With the bench drill press and appropriate forstner bit, bore out the various round windows. Glue the walls (A, E, F and G) together and fix with the 20 mm panel pins. Screw the inside floors (L and K) in place, ensuring everything is square.

Step 4: Painting and fitting Paint the whole work inside and out. Use sandpaper to rub down the paint and achieve an aged effect. Paint with varnish.

Step 5: Fixing the wire mesh Use the staples to hold the wire mesh (O) in place. When you come to the top bunker, bend the wire mesh round in a continuous curve – so that the single piece forms the bottom of the bunker as well as covering the round window holes. Hold the staples with the long-nose pliers and hammer them in.

Step 6: Fixing the roof Glue and pin one of the top roof flaps (B) (the other is hinged), glue and pin the middle roof flaps (C) and fix the bottom flaps with hinges. Use glue and pins to make the platform (H, I and J).

MOUNTING

Bang one of the posts (P) into the ground, and fix the platform to the top with the 80 mm nails and the claw hammer. Screw the feeder house to the platform. Cut the other post into four equal lengths and nail these in place under the platform, making a bracketed structure. Nail the dowel rod (N) to the main post.

CARVED DECOY DUCK RAFT FEEDER

Traditionally, the whole idea of the carved decoy duck is that you stake it out at the side of a lake, wait for real ducks to be attracted, jump up with your gun, and... bang, you have food for the pot! With this project, you simply forget the "bang" bit, and enjoy the delightful sight of ducks feeding around the decoy and its raft.

DESIGN NOTES

Duck carving is easier than it looks. You must choose a straight-grained wood that is easy to carve. We used English lime, but you could just as well pick American basswood or even some species of straight-grained pine – as long as the wood cuts easily and comes from a sustainable source. We favour using a bandsaw for cutting out the blank, a flat chisel for cutting the mortise, and a straight gouge and a knife for the modelling.

Materials
- Lime, 314 mm long, 100 mm thick and 150 mm wide (A)
- Lime, 134 mm long, 42 mm thick and 108 mm wide (B)
- 2 x pine posts, 660 mm long and 60 mm in diameter (C)
- 2 x pine boards, 600 mm long, 25 mm thick and 230 mm wide (D)
- Exterior-grade PVA wood glue
- Nails, 65 mm
- Water-based drawing inks, yellow, viridian, vermilion, peat brown and black
- Tracing paper
- Exterior-quality matt varnish

Tools
- Workbench with vice and holdfast
- Pencil, ruler, square and compass
- Scroll saw
- Paring chisel, 30 mm
- Sash clamp
- Carving mallets, heavyweight and lightweight
- Straight gouge, 25 mm wide
- Knife
- Sandpaper and sanding block
- Artist's watercolour brushes, fine, medium and large
- Paintbrush, 25 mm
- Claw hammer

DUCK TRAP

The original "decoy" was a large device made from wood and netting, used by hunters to trap wild ducks. However, the word can also refer to model ducks placed in the decoy to lure down wild birds, trapping them for food or to lay eggs.

The practice was originally Dutch – indeed the word "decoy" is derived from a Dutch word meaning "duck trap". The use of decoys soon spread throughout northern Europe, and was especially popular during the sixteenth and seventeenth centuries, with more than two hundred decoys built in England alone. The practice gradually died out, and today the few remaining decoys are used for scientific research.

Today, wooden decoy ducks can be used either to attract wild ducks to a garden pond, or simply to provide an attractive decorative feature in the garden. They can be left natural, or painted to resemble wild duck species.

The duck on our raft feeder is based on the commonest and best-known "wild duck" in north-west Europe – the Mallard. The male Mallard is one of the most handsome and distinctive of ducks, with a bottle-green head and dark magenta breast. Mallards are usually found in freshwater habitats such as lakes, but may visit small garden ponds, or even graze on a damp lawn.

Other waterbirds, such as the Moorhen, are regular visitors to gardens near lakes or ponds, especially during winter weather, when usual sources of water are iced over.

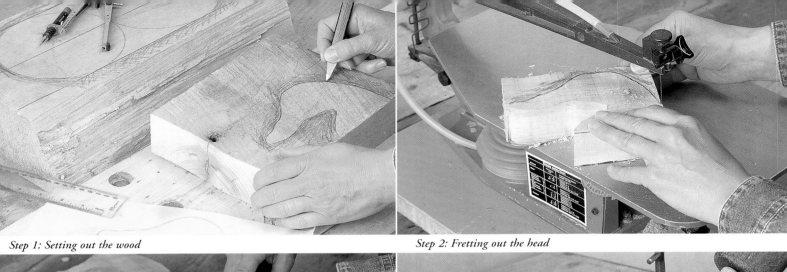

Step 1: Setting out the wood

Step 2: Fretting out the head

Step 3: Cutting the mortise

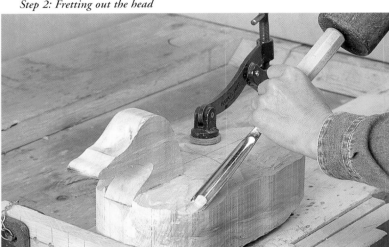

Step 4: Roughing out

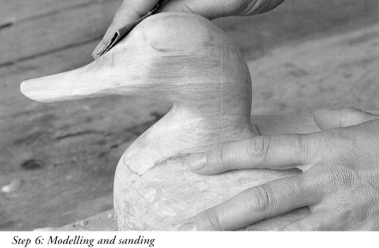

Step 6: Modelling and sanding

Step 5: Carving the form

Step 7: Painting and finishing

CONSTRUCTION DETAILS FOR THE CARVED DECOY DUCK RAFT FEEDER

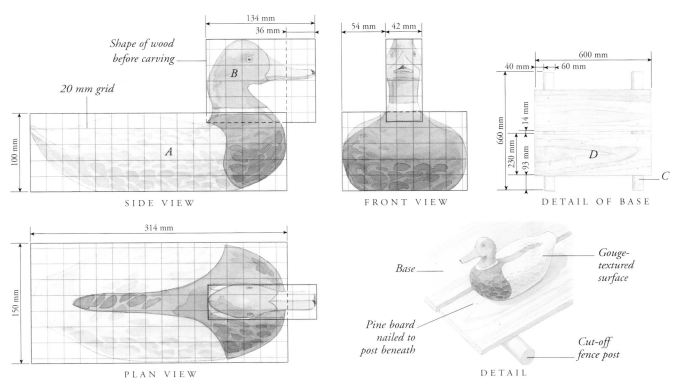

SIDE VIEW

FRONT VIEW

DETAIL OF BASE

PLAN VIEW

DETAIL

Shape of wood before carving

20 mm grid

Gouge-textured surface

Base

Pine board nailed to post beneath

Cut-off fence post

HOW TO MAKE THE PROJECT

Step 1: Setting out the wood Use the ruler and compass to set out the body slab (A) – 314 mm long, with a 57 mm radius at each end. Trace the head image (use the grid for guidance) on to the 42 mm-thick slab (B).

Step 2: Fretting out the head Fret out the head profile on the scroll saw. Work at a steady pace, with the line of cut always slightly to the waste side of the drawn line.

Step 3: Cutting the mortise Draw out the mortise at 84 mm long, 14 mm deep and 42 mm wide. Use the paring chisel to cut it out.

Step 4: Roughing out Secure the workpiece with the holdfast and the sash clamp, and use the heavyweight mallet and gouge to round over all the sawn corners.

Step 5: Carving the form Use the lightweight mallet and gouge to carve the form as shown in the front, side and plan views. Only cut in the direction of the grain.

Step 6: Modelling and sanding When you have achieved a good form – with the surface nicely dappled with gouge and knife cuts – use the sandpaper to rub down the duck to a smooth finish.

Step 7: Painting and finishing Use the watercolour brushes to lay on thin washes of colour: yellow for the bill, viridian for the head, a mix of vermilion and peat brown for the breast, and black for the eyes. When it is dry, use sandpaper to rub through the ink to reveal the underlying wood. Brush on a coat of matt varnish. Finally, set the two 660 mm posts (C) about 400 mm apart and nail the boards (D) in place with the claw hammer. If the nail points protrude, hammer them over.

MOUNTING

Choose a sheltered position at the water's edge, and set the raft and the duck in place. If you are worried about losing the duck – to predatory children – you could screw it to the raft and fix the whole work with stakes.

FOLK ART FEEDER HOUSE

This unusual and decorative bird house-cum-feeder table has been inspired by the American folk art of the eighteenth and nineteenth centuries. The gabled roof, wide balconies, arched doorways, heavy shutters, hooped balustrade and distressed paint finish make it slightly kitsch, with just a dash of New Orleans.

DESIGN NOTES

While this house may be viewed as "over the top" – it is perhaps overly large, too colourful, and just a tad too decorative – it is for all that a very successful design. The bright, eye-catching colours seem to attract the birds, the house provides shelter, and the hooped balustrade prevents the food from rolling off the balconies. From the human perspective, the whole house is simply good fun, and much favoured by children and adults alike. If you enjoy challenging woodwork, like decoration, and want a large splash of colour in the garden, then this is a project you can revel in. While at first sight the design looks somewhat difficult – all those bits and pieces coming together at different angles – it is in fact quite simple to make.

Materials

- Exterior plywood, 600 mm long, 9 mm thick and 600 mm wide (A)
- Exterior plywood, 500 mm long, 9 mm thick and 500 mm wide (B)
- 4 x pieces of exterior plywood, 560 mm long, 9 mm thick and 352 mm wide (C)
- 4 x pieces of exterior plywood, 428 mm long, 5 mm thick and 292 mm wide (D)
- 4 x wooden balls, about 40 mm in diameter (E)
- 5 mm threaded rod, 300 mm long, with two nuts and two washers (F)
- Rattan, 17 m length (G)
- Plastic lid, about 80 mm in diameter
- Exterior-grade PVA wood glue
- Panel pins, 12 mm
- Acrylic paint, white, brick red, mid-green and ochre
- Artist's oil paint, burnt umber
- Exterior-quality matt varnish
- Wire or rope to hang

Tools

- Workbench with vice
- Pencil, ruler and compass
- Engineer's square
- Crosscut saw
- Scroll saw with fine blade
- Pin hammer
- Paintbrush, 25 mm
- Sandpaper and sanding block
- Electric drill
- Twist drill bit, 3 mm
- Long-nose pliers and wire snips

PEANUT FEEDERS

A peanut feeder will attract a wide variety of birds to your garden. The rigid wire mesh design allows birds to take a firm grip, so they can peck off morsels of peanut (small birds could choke on whole nuts). Hang it from the base of your feeder house or bird table, or if you prefer, from a post or tree in a suitable position.

Peanut feeders are suitable for a wide range of species, especially tits, sparrows and finches such as the Greenfinch and Siskin. Good-quality peanuts are packed full of energy, allowing the birds to make the most of the limited time available for feeding during the short winter days, and increasing their chances of survival.

During harsh winter weather, you may need to replenish the feeder several times a day, though when natural food is plentiful it can last several weeks. Try experimenting with different coloured feeders: although most human beings like subtle colours such as green, it seems that birds prefer bright blue, red or silver!

CONSTRUCTION DETAILS FOR THE FOLK ART FEEDER HOUSE

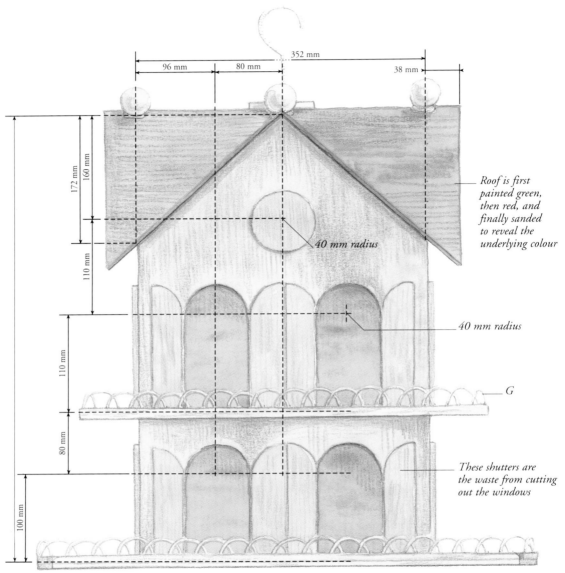

352 mm

96 mm   80 mm   38 mm

172 mm
160 mm
110 mm

110 mm

80 mm

100 mm

Roof is first painted green, then red, and finally sanded to reveal the underlying colour

40 mm radius

40 mm radius

G

These shutters are the waste from cutting out the windows

FRONT VIEW

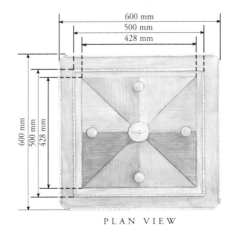

600 mm
500 mm
428 mm

600 mm
500 mm
428 mm

PLAN VIEW

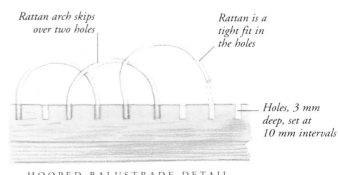

Rattan arch skips over two holes

Rattan is a tight fit in the holes

Holes, 3 mm deep, set at 10 mm intervals

HOOPED BALUSTRADE DETAIL

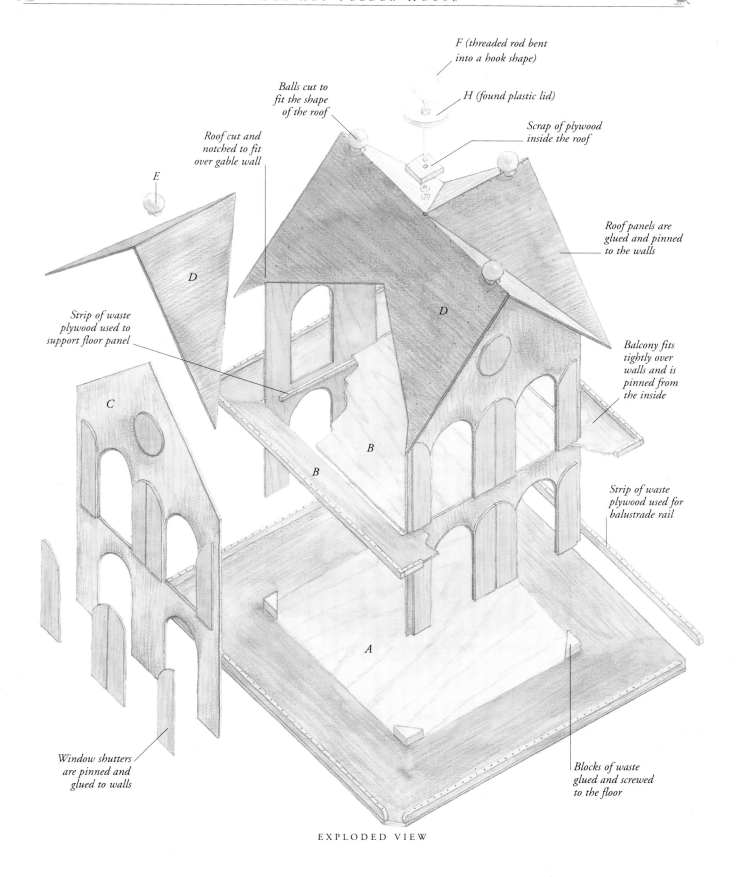

F (threaded rod bent into a hook shape)

H (found plastic lid)

Balls cut to fit the shape of the roof

Scrap of plywood inside the roof

Roof cut and notched to fit over gable wall

E

D

Roof panels are glued and pinned to the walls

D

Strip of waste plywood used to support floor panel

C

B

B

B

Balcony fits tightly over walls and is pinned from the inside

Strip of waste plywood used for balustrade rail

A

Window shutters are pinned and glued to walls

Blocks of waste glued and screwed to the floor

EXPLODED VIEW

Step 1: Setting out the design

Step 2: Fretting out the design

Step 3: Pinning the walls

Step 4: Fitting the roof

Step 5: Fixing the floor and first coat of paint

Step 6: Rubbing and texturing

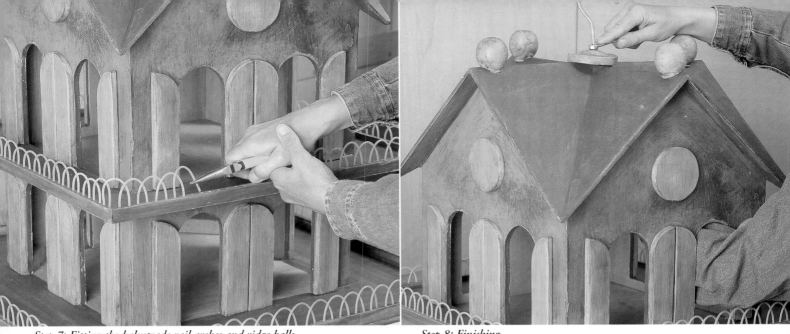

Step 7: Fitting the balustrade rail arches and ridge balls

Step 8: Finishing

HOW TO MAKE THE PROJECT

Step 1: Setting out the design Study the design and consider how the components best fit the plywood – to minimize wastage. Use the pencil, compass, engineer's square and ruler to set out the various parts.

Step 2: Fretting out the design Use the crosscut saw and the scroll saw to cut out the pieces. In the knowledge that the door-window waste becomes the shutters, run the line of cut straight up the door-window centre-line, from the bottom of the wall up to the head of the top window.

Step 3: Pinning the walls Mitre the corners of the walls (C) on the scroll saw. Smear glue on the 45° faces, join, and fix with the panel pins.

Step 4: Fitting the roof Fit the two long roof boards (D), and cut the other two roof boards (D) to fit. Glue and pin the roof panels to the walls.

Step 5: Fixing the floor and first coat of paint Cut the floors (A and B) to size and fix them in place with the 12 mm panel pins. Construct the raised balustrade strips from offcuts, and glue and pin them in place around the edge of the balustrade and the main floor. Paint everything white, and when dry, add further coats of paint as follows. Roof: green, outer walls: red, floors: green, balustrades: green, shutters and decorations: ochre.

Step 6: Rubbing and texturing When the paint is dry, use the sandpaper to carefully rub away areas of paint to expose the white underneath. Paint on a third coat of paint – roof: red, outer walls: green, floors: red, balustrades: red, shutters and decorations: ochre – and repeat the sanding procedure. Glue the shutters and discs in place. Mix a little artist's oil paint into the varnish. Paint all the surfaces, inside and out, with varnish.

Step 7: Fitting the balustrade rail arches and ridge balls Drill 3 mm holes at 10 mm intervals along the top of the balustrade strips. Use wire snips to cut the rattan (G) into 100 mm lengths, and the long-nose pliers to push it into the holes with the arches overlapping (each arch skips two holes). Glue the balls (E) in place on the ridge, and give them a coat of the burnt umber varnish.

Step 8: Finishing With the pliers, bend the threaded rod into a hook shape (F) and run it down through the plastic lid (H) and the roof. Spread the load by having a piece of scrap plywood on the inside. Fix with the washers and nuts.

MOUNTING

Select a suitable site, such as a stout branch or a garden structure. Use wire or rope to hang the house about 2 metres from the ground.

EDWARDIAN-STYLE DOVECOTE

Nothing evokes the English cottage garden quite so well as a dovecote. Painted white and mounted high up on a gable, the cote provides a safe haven not only for doves but for all manner of birds. Just imagine a warm summer's evening, the sun low in the sky, with doves slowly circling, about to come to roost – wonderful!

DESIGN NOTES

This design looks quite complicated – lots of fancy brackets, arched doors, landing platforms, all topped off with a roof finial – but it is in fact a relatively straightforward project. The forms are cut out with a hand-held portable jigsaw and a bench scroll saw, waste pieces are cleverly used as trim, most of it is made from 9 mm exterior plywood, and the making stages are surprisingly easy. There is no complicated chisel work or joint cutting and the whole project is put together with screws.

LOVE DOVES

Birds have been kept and bred in captivity since time immemorial. One of the most popular groups of birds amongst aviculturists is that of pigeons and doves. They are attractive, easily tamed, and breed throughout the year, enabling many varieties to be produced by artificial selection, such as the exotic-looking Fantail Pigeon.

Descendants of the wild Rock Dove also have excellent homing abilities, enabling them to be used for racing, or for carrying messages. During the Second World War, many British and Allied servicemen owed their lives to messages delivered by carrier pigeons.

Pigeons and doves are kept in lofts, or dovecotes, of which this is an ornamental version designed as an attractive item of garden furniture. It is unlikely that wild birds would use the dovecote, although you might try putting out seed on the ledges to attract the familiar Collared Dove.

Materials

- 2 x pieces exterior plywood, 900 mm long, 9 mm thick and 600 mm wide (A) (B)
- 2 x pieces exterior plywood, 798 mm long, 9 mm thick and 300 mm wide (C)
- 3 x pieces exterior plywood, 582 mm long, 9 mm thick and 300 mm wide (D)(E)(F)
- Exterior plywood, 564 mm long, 9 mm thick and 188 mm wide (G)
- Exterior plywood, 564 mm long, 9 mm thick and 234 mm wide (H)
- 2 x pieces exterior plywood, 196 mm long, 9 mm thick and 168 mm wide (I)
- 4 x pieces exterior plywood, 134 mm long, 9 mm thick and 105 mm wide (J)
- 2 x pieces exterior plywood, 240 mm long, 9 mm thick and 72 mm wide (K)
- Pine, 180 mm long, 36 x 36 mm square section (L)
- 2 x pieces exterior plywood, 420 mm long, 9 mm thick and 408 mm wide (M)
- 10 x pieces pine feather-edge board, 408 mm long, 13 mm thick and 84 mm wide (N)
- 5 x pieces sawn pine, 90 mm long, 25 mm thick and 51 mm wide (O)
- Sawn pine, 25 x 25 mm square section:
  6 x 300 mm long (P),
  4 x 120 mm long (Q),
  3 x 532 mm long (R) and
  4 x 65 mm long (S)
- Matt white exterior paint
- Clear exterior-quality varnish
- Exterior-grade PVA wood glue
- Screws, 16 mm and 25 mm
- Long screws or bolts

Tools

- Workbench with vice and holdfast
- Pencil, ruler, square and compass
- Hand-held jigsaw
- Electric drill with a good selection of twist bits
- Screwdrivers
- Paintbrush, 25 mm
- Crosscut saw
- Scroll saw

CONSTRUCTION DETAILS FOR THE EDWARDIAN-STYLE DOVECOTE

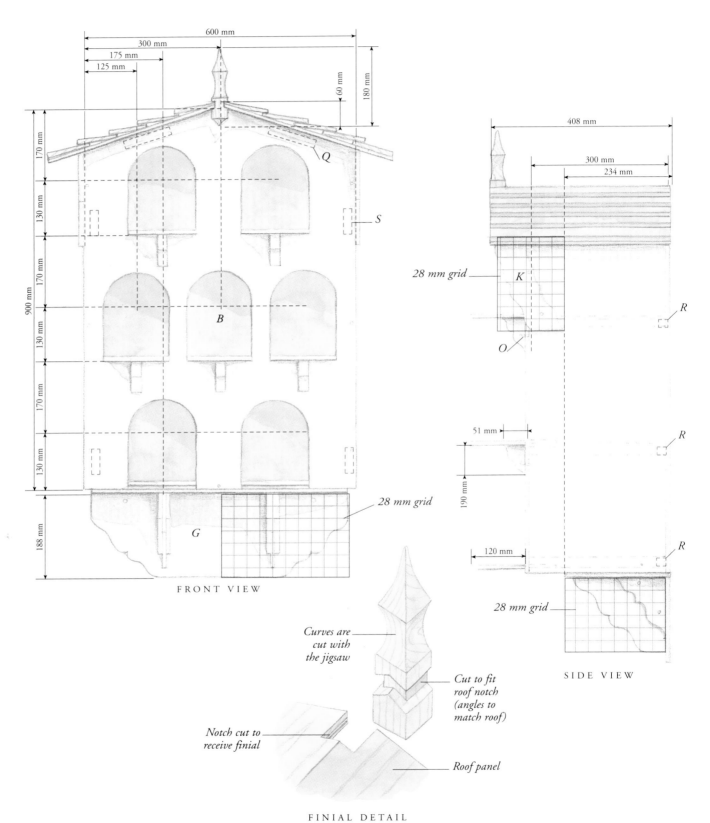

FRONT VIEW

600 mm
300 mm
175 mm
125 mm
60 mm
180 mm
170 mm
130 mm
900 mm
170 mm
130 mm
170 mm
130 mm
188 mm

Q

S

B

G

28 mm grid

SIDE VIEW

408 mm
300 mm
234 mm

28 mm grid

K

O

R

R

R

51 mm
190 mm
120 mm

28 mm grid

FINIAL DETAIL

Curves are cut with the jigsaw

Cut to fit roof notch (angles to match roof)

Roof panel

Notch cut to receive finial

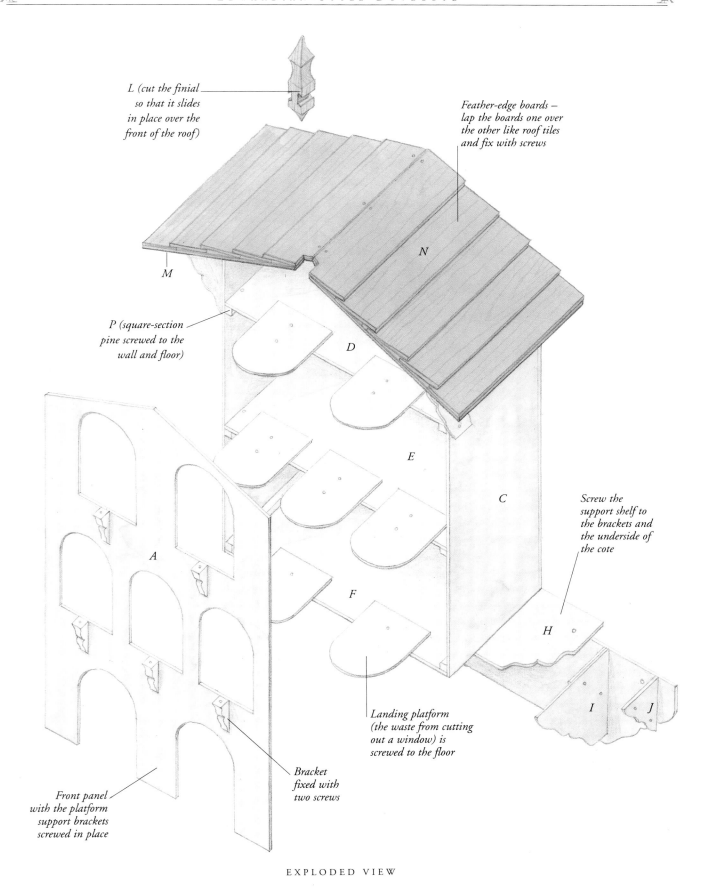

L (cut the finial so that it slides in place over the front of the roof)

Feather-edge boards – lap the boards one over the other like roof tiles and fix with screws

N

M

P (square-section pine screwed to the wall and floor)

D

E

C

Screw the support shelf to the brackets and the underside of the cote

A

F

H

I

J

Landing platform (the waste from cutting out a window) is screwed to the floor

Bracket fixed with two screws

Front panel with the platform support brackets screwed in place

EXPLODED VIEW

Step 1: Setting out the design

Step 2: Using the jigsaw

Step 3: Fixing the first side, floors, back and platforms

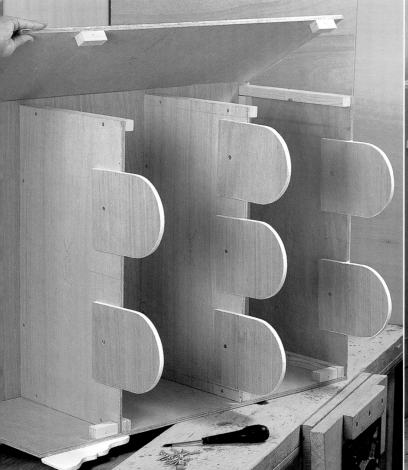

Step 4: Fitting the second side

Step 5: Fixing the front and roof boards

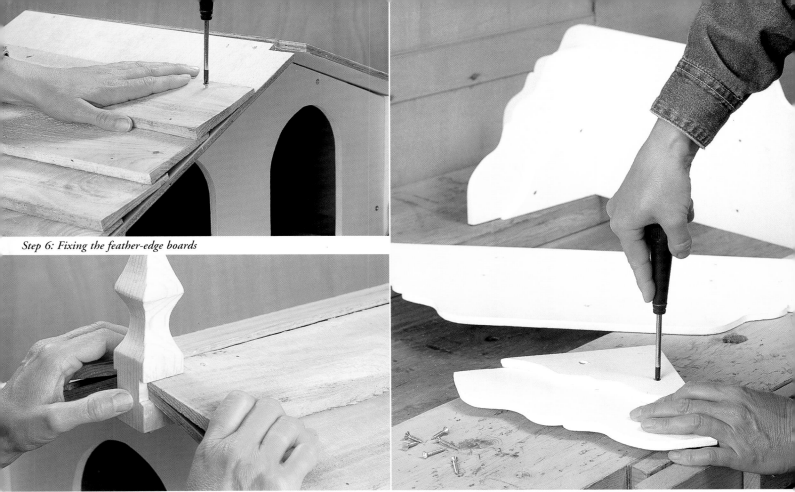

Step 6: Fixing the feather-edge boards

Step 7: Fixing the finial

Step 8: Making and fitting the support brackets

HOW TO MAKE THE PROJECT

Step 1: Setting out the design Use the pencil, ruler, square and compass to set out the panels.

Step 2: Using the jigsaw Cut out the door holes. Drill a starting hole on the bottom edge of the enclosed doors.

Step 3: Fixing the first side, floors, back and platforms Fit the first side (C), back (B) and the floors (D, E and F) together with battens (P, Q, R and S). Paint the underside of the platforms and screw them to the floors.

Step 4: Fitting the second side Screw the second side into place with the 25 mm screws.

Step 5: Fixing the front and roof boards Screw the roof boards (M) in place, and the brackets (O) to the front board. Paint and varnish the whole work. Screw the front (A) to the side boards with the 25 mm screws and screw the platforms to the brackets.

Step 6: Fixing the feather-edge boards Saw the feather-edge boards (N) to length with the crosscut saw, lap them one over the other and fix with the 16 mm screws.

Step 7: Fixing the finial Cut the finial (L) to shape with the scroll saw and then notch each side so that it slides in place on the front edge of the roof. Fix with glue.

Step 8: Making and fitting the support brackets Paint the component parts that make up the support shelf – the back board (G), the top board (H) and the angles (I and J). Fix them together with glue and the 16 mm screws. Finally, glue and screw (with the 16 mm screws) the support shelf to the underside of the dovecote.

MOUNTING

Find a position high up on a gable, under the eaves, or on a shed. Fix the dovecote about 3–4 metres above the ground, using long screws or bolts.

CONVERSION TABLE

To convert the metric measurements given in this book to imperial measurements, simply multiply the figure given in the text by the relevant number shown in the table below. Bear in mind that conversions will not necessarily work out exactly, and you will need to round the figure up or down slightly. (Do not use a combination of metric and imperial measurements – for accuracy, keep to one system.)

To convert	Multiply by
millimetres to inches	0.0394
metres to feet	3.28
metres to yards	1.093
sq millimetres to sq inches	0.00155
sq metres to sq feet	10.76

To convert	Multiply by
sq metres to sq yards	1.195
cu metres to cu feet	35.31
cu metres to cu yards	1.308
grams to pounds	0.0022
kilograms to pounds	2.2046

USEFUL ADDRESSES

UK CONTACTS

RSPB (The Royal Society for the Protection of Birds), The Lodge, Sandy, Bedfordshire SG19 2DI

YOC (Young Ornithologists Club), The Lodge, Sandy, Bedfordshire SG19 2DI

BTO (British Trust for Ornithology), The National Centre for Ornithology, The Nunnery, Thetford, Norfolk IP24 2PU

SOUTH AFRICAN CONTACTS

BirdLife South Africa, P O Box 515, Randburg 2125, South Africa

Ornithological Association of Zimbabwe, P O Box 8382, Causeway, Zimbabwe

Botswana Bird Club, P O Box 71, Gaborone, Botswana

Namibian Bird Club, P O Box 67, Windhoek, Namibia

UK BIRD FOOD SUPPLIERS

CJ Wildbird Foods Ltd., The Rea, Upton Magna, Shrewsbury SY4 4UB

John E. Haith Ltd., Park Street, Cleethorpes, Humberside DN35 7NF

Jayne Jacobi & Co., Hawthorn Cottage, Maypole, Hoath, Canterbury, Kent CT3 4LW

SOUTH AFRICAN BIRD FOOD SUPPLIERS

Bird Man Pets, Shoprite Shopping Centre, Van Riebeeck Street, Kuils River 7580

Pet City, Wonderwater Centre, Cnr Braam Pretorius & Lavender Streets, Wonderboom, Pretoria 0182

Pet Emporium, 7 Berea Centre, Berea Road, Berea, Durban

Kempton Pets Paradise, 64 Main Street, Brentwood Park, Johannesburg

Samuel Hardy Ironmongery, Freepost 824, York YO1 1AG. Tel: 0500 767 770 (toll-free)

South London Hardwoods, 12 Belgrave Rd, London SE25 5AN. Tel: 020 8771 6764

Stanley Tools, The Stanley Works, Woodside, Sheffield S3 9PD

UK WOODWORKING SUPPLIERS

Axminster Power Tool Centre, Chard Street, Axminster, Devon EX13 5DZ

De Walt Tools, 210 Bath Rd, Slough SL1 3YD

John Boddy's Fine Wood and Tool Store Ltd., Riverside Saw Mills, Boroughbridge, North Yorkshire YO5 9LJ

North Heighham Sawmills Ltd, Paddock St, Norfolk NR2 4TW. Tel: 01603 622 978

SOUTH AFRICAN WOODWORKING SUPPLIERS

Federated Timbers
Cape Town: Plantation Road, Wetton 7780
Johannesburg: 128 Plane Road, Kempton Park 1619
Durban: 11 Bishop Road, Pinetown 3610
Bloemfontein: 14a MacKenzie Street, 9301

FURTHER READING

Attracting Birds to Your Garden, STEPHEN MOSS AND DAVID COTTRIDGE, New Holland, UK, 1998

Chris Packham's Back Garden Nature Reserve, New Holland, UK, Available: April 2001

Bill Oddie's Birds of Britain and Ireland, New Holland, UK, 1999

The Bird Table Book, TONY SOPER, David and Charles, UK, 1992

Creating a Wildlife Garden, BOB AND LIZ GIBBONS, Hamlyn, UK, 1988

Feed the Birds, TONY SOPER, David and Charles, UK, 1991

The Nature Observer's Handbook, JOHN W. BRAINERD, Globe Pequot Press, USA, 1986

Attracting Backyard Wildlife, WILLIAM J. MERILLEES, Voyager Press, USA, 1989

Garden Bird Facts, MARCUS SCHNECK, Barnes and Noble Books, USA, 1992

Hosting the Birds, JAN MAHNKEN, Storey Books, USA, 1989

The Natural Garden, KEN DRUSE, Clarkson, USA, 1989

INDEX

PHOTOGRAPH ACKNOWLEDGEMENTS
David Cottridge pp: 6, 8, 9, 10, 12, 13, 15, 16(r), 17; Richard Revels p 16(bl); Paul Sterry p 16(tl)